THE LOUISIANA PURCHASE

AMERICAN OCCUPATION

THE

LOUISIANA PURCHASE
AND THE EXPLORATION
EARLY HISTORY AND
BUILDING OF
THE WEST

BY

RIPLEY HITCHCOCK

With Illustrations
and Maps

BOSTON, U.S.A.

GINN & COMPANY, PUBLISHERS

The Athenæum Press

1903

THE LOUISIANA PURCHASE

By Ripley Hitchcock

As Published in 1903

Trade Paperback ISBN: 1-58218-236-1
Hardcover ISBN: 1-58218-237-X
eBook ISBN: 1-58218-235-3

Digital Scanning and Publishing is a leader in the electronic republication of historical books and documents. We publish many of our titles as eBooks, as well as traditional hardcover and trade paper editions. DSI is committed to bringing many traditional and little known books back to life, retaining the look and feel of the original work.

©2001 DSI Digital Reproduction
First DSI Printing: March 2001

Published by DIGITAL SCANNING, INC.
Scituate, MA 02066
www.digitalscanning.com

TO

M. W. H.

INTRODUCTION

In the year 1803 the United States bought from France the greater part of our country lying between the Mississippi River and the Rocky Mountains. The area acquired contained nearly a million square miles. This "Louisiana Purchase" has been called an event "worthy to rank with the Declaration of Independence and the formation of the Constitution."

The price of the empire which we gained in 1803 was $15,000,000. This seems a large amount even in this day of the easy handling of millions, but the taxable wealth of the Louisiana territory to-day is more than four hundred times the purchase money. In whole or in part fourteen states and territories have been formed in the area which was bought, and there are over fifteen million people within its borders.

These are impressive facts and they invite questions as to what the Louisiana territory was and how we happened to secure it. The answers tell a curious story, full of happenings so strange that they have the quality of romance. In the sixteenth century the Spaniards, first of white men to penetrate Louisiana, might have occupied and perhaps have held it for at least two centuries and a half, but they were lured away by the gold and silver of Mexico and South America. Later there were disasters near home, and always there was their own incapacity in colonization.

Next came the French, descending from the north and holding Louisiana until their power on this continent was broken at the fall of Quebec in 1759. Four years later France ceded Louisiana to Spain. After our Revolution England yielded us a boundary on the Great Lakes, the Mississippi, and the thirty-first degree. She promised also the free navigation of the Mississippi. But this promise Spain, holding the river's mouth, refused to sanction, and as American pioneers pressed westward across the Alleghenies and sought the natural route to a market afforded by the water ways, this refusal became a matter of supreme moment.

There followed a critical period in the history of the West. In 1790 the possibility of a war between England and Spain led Pitt to consider a seizure of New Orleans. A little later France, always regretting the loss of Louisiana, employed the French minister Genet to use the discontent of our frontiersmen as a means of wresting Louisiana and Florida from Spain. Later still France's efforts to regain Louisiana became successful under the powerful guidance of Napoleon. His plans were laid for occupation. They were checked by the negro revolt in San Domingo and the prospect of war with England.

Meantime the West was ablaze, and President Jefferson sent Monroe as commissioner to Paris to secure New Orleans and the Floridas and make clear the way to the sea. The instructions of Monroe and Livingston were limited to a strip of seacoast. But

Napoleon changed his mind. He offered them the whole vast area of Louisiana, and thus suddenly and unexpectedly we acquired Louisiana from France even before possession had formally passed to France from Spain.

What was bought was for the most part a wilderness. How this wilderness was explored is told in the second part of this volume in an abridged version of the journals of Lewis and Clark, the classical explorers of the West.

This outline of the first great American expedition into the far West and across the continent is followed by sketches of the journeys of Pike, Colton, Hunt, Wyeth, Prince Maximilian of Wied, Bonneville, Frémont, and others,—soldiers, traders, scientists, makers of the old trails, and pioneers of the greatest of river routes, the Missouri-Mississippi. This third division of the story naturally includes the American fur trade, as well as the trails and water routes of the West. These explorers, trappers, and traders made the early American history of Louisiana, but long before them were the eras of Spaniards like Coronado, and Frenchmen like Father Marquette, La Salle, and the Verendryes.

The waning of the fur trade's supremacy toward the middle of the nineteenth century was followed by discoveries of mineral wealth, by the pressure of settlement, by railroad building, by the cattle industry, and by other factors in the earlier building of the West which are sketched in the fourth part of this narrative. With the later political organization and giant growth of the old Louisiana territory within comparatively recent years this history deals only in a summary of facts.

Since the purpose of this book is to afford a continuous and very simple narrative, it has not seemed necessary or wise to enter at length into the diplomatic and political history of the purchase of Louisiana. That story may be read in the first and second volumes of Henry Adams's "History of the United States of America" and in McMaster's "History of the People of the United States." The French side of the history is emphasized in

Dr. J. K. Hosmer's popular "History of the Louisiana Purchase." Many other references will be found throughout this volume.

There seems to be no single book which tells the story of the West succinctly and includes the work of the Spanish and French pioneers, and also accounts of the various phases of American exploration and of the typical figures and aspects of the Western formative periods. It is hoped that this volume, in spite of its modest character, may afford a certain comprehensiveness which will be of convenience and of value to students of the earlier history of the West between the Mississippi and the mountains.

I desire to express my sense of obligation to my friends, Professor John Bach McMaster and George Parker Winship, Esq., for their kindness in reading portions of the proofs. I wish also to acknowledge the aid of Mr. Percy Waller of the Lenox Library, New York, in reading the proofs and in preparing the index.

R. H.

CONTENTS

PART I

DISCOVERY AND ACQUISITION

THE SPANISH AND FRENCH PERIODS AND THE
PURCHASE

xi

CONTENTS

CONTENTS xiii

PART II

THE LEWIS AND CLARK EXPEDITION

CONTENTS

PART III

THE EXPLORATION OF THE WEST

PART IV

THE BUILDING OF THE WEST

LIST OF ILLUSTRATIONS AND MAPS

ILLUSTRATIONS AND MAPS xxi

LOUISIANA

═══

PART I

DISCOVERY AND ACQUISITION

THE SPANISH AND FRENCH PERIODS
AND
THE PURCHASE

Map showing the Expansion of the United States on this Continent, omitting Alaska

CHAPTER I

THE SPANISH DISCOVERERS

What the Louisiana Purchase was. Early Spanish explorers. Discovery of the Mississippi. Pineda, Cabeza de Vaca, Coronado, De Soto, and Docampo. The Spaniards first in the field. Their weakness in colonization.

At the opening of the year 1803 the territory of the United States was bounded on the west by the Mississippi River.[1] In April of that year a treaty was signed in Paris by which nearly a million square miles west of the Mississippi, stretching from the mouth of the river to British America, was purchased from France for $15,000,000, and the total area of our country was more than doubled. This great event is known in history as the

[1]On the south the boundary was the thirty-first parallel of latitude from the Mississippi to the Apalachicola, down the middle of that river to the Flint, thence to the head of St. Marys River, and down the latter to the sea.

3

Louisiana Purchase. By this treaty, which was signed by Robert R. Livingston and James Monroe representing the United States, and Barbé-Marbois representing the Republic of France, Napoleon Bonaparte—then the First Consul of France and afterward Emperor—ceded to the United States the territory which now contains Louisiana, Arkansas, Kansas, Missouri, Iowa, Nebraska, South Dakota, North Dakota, Montana, Wyoming, Indian Territory, and parts of Colorado and Oklahoma.[1]

[1]Much attention has been given by historians to the question whether or not Texas was or should have been included in the Louisiana Purchase. Henry Adams and Professor Edward Channing are among the more conspicuous advocates of Texas as a part of Louisiana, and Professor A. C. McLaughlin declares that France "had good ground for claiming the Texas country perhaps even to the Rio Grande." Schouler and H. H. Bancroft take a contrary view, and the thesis that Texas was not a part of the Louisiana Purchase is ably maintained in an interesting monograph by Professor John R. Ficklen. This discussion is not essential to the present narrative, since the United States, after claiming the territory as far west not only as the Rio Bravo but even to the Rio Grande, yielded the point in 1819, when by treaty with Spain the Floridas were acquired and Texas abandoned.

It is easy now to see that this great addition to our country was of incalculable importance. At the time, however, the significance of the purchase, which has been called a turning point in our history, was not realized. We can understand the situation better by showing what had been learned up to 1803 of the vast region which Jefferson and Napoleon added to the United States.

It is sometimes said that the Louisiana territory was unexplored. In one sense this is true, but we shall find that as a matter of fact many white men had penetrated this wilderness. The first were Spaniards who followed after Columbus. The purpose of Columbus, and, for a time, of others after him, was to find a water way to Cathay, or China, and the Spice Islands by the westward route, and to secure their rich trade. The extent of America was so little understood that much time was spent in trying to find a passage through or around our continent. Cipango, as Japan was called, was supposed to lie much farther east; indeed, in some old maps it seems included within our boundaries. It was the Spanish pioneer explorers of the sixteenth century who first penetrated western North America and discovered the vast extent of our country.

It was in a search for this water route to the west that, in 1519, Don Diego Velasquez, the Spanish governor of Cuba, sent out four caravels commanded by Don Alonzo Alvarez de Pineda. The little fleet finally sailed westward across the Gulf of Mexico until Pineda met Cortes, the conqueror of Mexico, and his followers, who claimed that territory. The point of chief interest to us is that on his return Pineda found the mouth of a great river, which he explored for a few leagues and named the *Rio de Espiritu Santo*. This was the Mississippi. We may think of Pineda, therefore, as the first white man to approach the confines of the territory known later as Louisiana.

A few years later, in 1527, another Spaniard reached Louisiana, and the story of this man, Alvar Nuñez Cabeza de Vaca,[1] is of peculiar

[1] The "Relation" of Cabeza de Vaca's journey, by himself, was first published at Zamora, Spain, in 1542. The

historical interest. He was treasurer of an expedition sent from Spain to Florida. With his comrades he struggled across Florida to the Gulf, and then, sorely tried by their hardships, they built rude boats as best they could. Their horses were killed for food. The manes and tails and some vegetable fibers were twisted into ropes; rough tools and nails were wrought out of stirrups and spurs, and shirts were pieced together for sails. Finally, the unhappy fugitives put to sea in five boats. They were ignorant of the waters and the coast, but they hoped to reach the Spanish settlements in Mexico. After a time they passed the mouth of the Mississippi, and then their boats were shattered by storms, and only fifteen men lived to be cast upon an island west of the mouth of the Mississippi, which they aptly termed "The Isle of Misfortunes."

first edition of Buckingham Smith's translation appeared in 1851, and the last, after his death, in 1871. While the translator's notes cannot be accepted implicitly in the light of later research, this translation holds a place of peculiar distinction in our early history as the first presentation in English of a most important source of historical knowledge.

Of this remnant all but four were slain by the Indians. Cabeza de Vaca himself was taken captive. For six terrible years he was held by his savage masters, who dwelt in eastern Texas and western Louisiana. Sometimes he was forced to act as a "medicine man." Again he was sent out as a trader, making long journeys as far north as the Red River country, where, it is believed, he was the first white man to see the "hunch-backed cows," as the older Spanish writers termed the buffalo. Finally, at some point west of the Sabine River in Texas, he was reunited to his three surviving comrades. They succeeded in escaping from their captors, and by using the rites of "medicine men," with which they mingled "earnest prayers to the true God," they preserved themselves from harm at the hands of other Indians.

Slowly and painfully they toiled westward across Texas, hoping to reach the Spaniards in Mexico. They seem to have crossed the Rio Pecos near its junction with the Rio Grande, and then crossing the latter river to have journeyed

Toreau
fauuage.

tre ceſte Floride & la riuiere de Palme ſe trouuent
diuerſes eſpeces de beſtes monſtrueuſes: entre leſquel-
les lon peut voir vne eſpece de grands taureaux, por-

tans cornes longues ſeulement d'vn pié, & ſur le dos
vne tumueur ou eminence, come vn chameau: le poil
long par tout le corps, duquel la couleur s'approche fort
de celle d'vne mule faue, & encores l'eſt plus celuy
qui eſt deſſoubs le mentõ. Lon en amena vne fois deux
tous viſs en Eſpagne, de l'vn deſquels j'ay veu la peau
& non autre choſe, & n'y peurent viure long temps.
Ceſt animal ainſi que lon dit, eſt perpetuel ennemy du
cheual, & ne le peut endurer pres de luy. De la Floride tirant au promontoire de Baxe, ſe trouue quelque
petite riuiere, ou les eſclaues vont peſcher huitres, qui
portent perles. Or depuis que ſommes venus iuſque là,
que de toucher la collection des huitres, ne veux ou-
blier par quel moyen les parles en ſont tirées, tant aux
Indes

Cap de
Baxe.

Huittes
portans
perles.

THE BUFFALO

(From Thevet's "Les Singularitez de la France Antarctique," Antwerp,
1558. Winsor considers this one of the earliest, if not the
earliest, picture of the buffalo.)

through the Mexican states of Chihuahua and
Sonora. Turning southward they finally, in
May, 1536, reached Culiacan in Sinaloa, the
northern outpost of Spanish settlement. Over
two thousand miles were traversed by these
fugitives in this flight, which restored them
to their countrymen eight years after their ill-
starred expedition landed in Florida.

With the exception of their passage by the
mouth of the Mississippi and some wanderings
in Louisiana and to the north, they had had
little to do with the actual territory of the
Purchase,[1] but the stories which these survivors
brought back made others eager to explore
the mysterious interior of the New World.

One story which appealed particularly to
the imaginations of the Spaniards was a tale
which Cabeza de Vaca had heard of the Seven
Cities of Cibola, to the north, which were described as full of treasures. In search of these
cities a fearless priest, Fray Marcos de Nizza,
started from Sinaloa in 1539, taking with him
one of Cabeza de Vaca's companions, a negro

[1]That is, of course, eliminating Texas.

named Estevanico. He found no treasures, but he reached the "cities," which are believed to have been the pueblos or villages of the Zuñi Indians near the present Zuñi village in western New Mexico.

When he returned and reported that he had actually seen certain strange towns to the north, there was a stir among the Spaniards, always tireless in the quest for treasure. The viceroy of Mexico, Mendoza, promptly organized an expedition under the command of Coronado, governor of New Galicia, to take possession of this rich country. He started in 1540, captured the Zuñi villages and wintered in New Mexico, where he heard a marvelous tale which brought destruction to many of the early treasure seekers. This was the legend of Quivira, a wonderful city of gold. Lured by this golden myth, Coronado crossed Indian Territory and pressed on to northeastern Kansas.[1]

[1]General Simpson believed that Coronado reached a point somewhere in the eastern half of the border country of Kansas and Nebraska. Bandelier placed the main seat of the Quiviras "in northeastern Kansas, beyond the Arkansas River and more than 100 miles northeast of Great Bend."

PUEBLO OF THE ZUNI INDIANS

(From a photograph)

He found a tribe of Indians called the Quiviras, but they had no gold and knew of none, and he was forced to make his painful way back empty-handed. This wonderful journey of Coronado may be called the first great exploration within the Louisiana territory.

It is most fortunate that narratives of this remarkable expedition have come down to us. The best of these was written by Castañeda, who is supposed to have been a well-educated private soldier in Coronado's army.[1]

A journey far longer and more perilous than that of Coronado originated in the devotion of the brave priest Fray Juan de Padilla, who was with Coronado, and returned to minister to the Quiviras accompanied only by one soldier, Andrés Docampo, and two boys, Lucas and Sebastian. The good priest was slain in northeastern Kansas. Docampo and the boys

[1]A translation of this narrative follows Mr. George Parker Winship's critical discussion of the Coronado expedition published in the Report of the Bureau of Ethnology for 1892–1893. "The Spanish Pioneers," by C. F. Lummis, offers a vivid sketch of early Spanish exploration and conquest throughout the Western Hemisphere.

wandered over the plains for nine heart-break-
ing years, sometimes prisoners, sometimes
fugitives, finally reaching the Mexican town of
Tampico on the Gulf. Their journeyings must
have covered thousands of miles of Louisiana
territory, but no records have been preserved.[1]

At the same time that Coronado was leading
his soldiers eastward, another Spanish officer
was struggling from Florida towards the west.
This was the famous Fernando de Soto, governor of Cuba, who was commissioned to conquer
the unknown territory on the Gulf of Mexico
which had been granted to Narvaez by a royal
patent. De Soto sailed from Havana in 1539
and, landing his force of nearly six hundred
men in Florida, fought his bloody way through
Georgia and Alabama and on to the Mississippi,
which he crossed at Chickasaw Bluff. This
was in 1541, and De Soto was the first white
man to see the Mississippi except at its mouth.[2]

[1]See "The Spanish Pioneers," by C. F. Lummis.

[2]There has been much historical discussion as to the discovery of the Mississippi, and the question of the claims of
Pineda in 1519, of Cabeza de Vaca, who crossed one of its
mouths in 1528, and of De Soto, has been argued at length

After crossing the great river De Soto marched
northward to Little Prairie, led by the vague

DE SOTO'S FIRST VIEW OF THE MISSISSIPPI RIVER

tales of gold which so often lured the Spaniards
to an evil fate. He sent out expeditions, one

by Rye in the Hakluyt Society's "Discovery and Conquest
of Florida," 1851. See Winsor's "Narrative and Critical
History of America," Vol. II, pp. 289-292.

of which marched eight days to the northwest and reached the open prairies. It seems
probable that De Soto approached the Missouri River, although he learned nothing of it.

At this very time, in the summer of 1541,
De Soto and his starving followers must have
been so near Coronado's army that an Indian
runner could have carried a message from one
to the other in a few days. Indeed, Coronado
heard of these white men and sent a messenger,
who failed in his errand. Thus, in the first
half of the sixteenth century two Spaniards,
one starting from Tampa Bay in Florida and
the other from the Gulf of California, practically completed a journey across the continent.[1]

De Soto's wanderings on the west bank of
the Mississippi are of interest here chiefly
because he entered the Louisiana territory.
He met with little save disaster, and after a
bitter winter passed on a branch of the Mississippi, which seems to have been the Washita,
he started southward with the remnants of

[1]Winsor's "Narrative and Critical History of America,"
Vol. II, p. 292.

his force. At the mouth of the Red River, on
May 21, 1542, the baffled "conqueror" died.
Surrounded as his survivors were by hostile
Indians, they dared not leave his body in a
grave lest the Indians should discover it; so

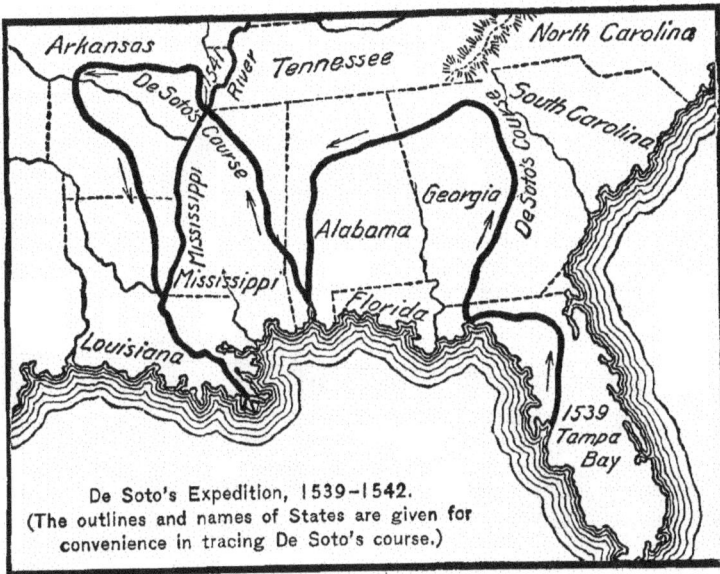

De Soto's Expedition, 1539–1542.
(The outlines and names of States are given for
convenience in tracing De Soto's course.)

this proud Spanish warrior found his last resting place beneath the waters of the Mississippi.

The survivors, led by Luis de Moscoço, at
first undertook to go westward in the hope of
reaching their countrymen in New Spain, and
some chroniclers have credited them with so

long a journey across the plains that they came within sight of the mountains. But their attempts to reach their friends in Mexico yielded no results, and they made their painful way back to the Mississippi. There they built boats and descended the river. They skirted the coast of Texas, and in September, 1543, the wretched remnants of De Soto's once proud expedition reached Tampico.

Pineda had found the mouth of the *Rio de Espiritu Santo,* but De Soto is justly remembered as the true discoverer of the Mississippi. On this discovery was based an early claim to Louisiana. But the story of the Spaniards in North America was very different from their record in the south, where Cortes had gained an empire by his conquest of Mexico (1519–1521), and Pizarro another in Peru (1531–1534). The early expeditions of the Spaniards within the present territory of the United States represented even larger possibilities, as they were the first comers in this new land.

Pineda, Coronado, De Soto, and other Spaniards made their journeys in the first half of the sixteenth century, and the oldest town in the United States, St. Augustine, Florida, was founded by the Spaniards in 1565. The Spaniards had sailed by the shores of Virginia long before Raleigh had dreamed of settlement.

OLD SPANISH GATEWAY AT ST. AUGUSTINE

It was not until 1605 that the French on the north founded Port Royal, now Annapolis, N. S., which was followed by Quebec in 1608. It was not until 1607 that the English founded Jamestown, in Virginia, and not until 1620 that the Pilgrims made their way to Plymouth. Thus in the struggle for a continent the Spaniards had all the advantages of priority, and they might have held North America. But Spanish discovery was not accompanied by the qualities which have wrought out a very different history for Anglo-Saxon expansion, and there were other obstacles.

Louisiana lay open to Spain in the sixteenth century, but the Spaniards, like other Europeans of their time, held to the "Bullion theory,"—that the precious metals were the only form of wealth,—and the gold and silver of Mexico and South America blinded them to the opportunities awaiting them in the development of the Mississippi valley. Furthermore, after 1570 Spain's energies were absorbed in attempts to suppress Protestantism in Europe and to crush the revolting Netherlands.[1] In 1588 Spain's maritime power was crippled by England's destruction of the Invincible Armada.

All this checked a career in the New World which, continuing as it began, might have

[1]See "The Discovery of America," by John Fiske, particularly Chapter XII.

meant a warfare against heretics in Virginia and New England like that which stained the early annals of Florida. It might have meant also an assured grasp of the Mississippi and

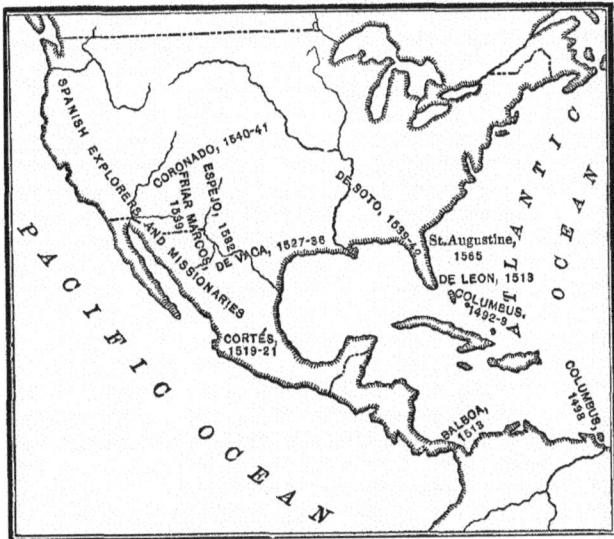

SPANISH EXPLORATIONS

Louisiana. But Spain's distraction and exhaustion gave a clear field for the English settlers on the eastern seaboard, and also for the French who came from the north to explore the Mississippi and claim the interior of our country.

The seventeenth century found Spain suspicious and uneasy, but for the most part

inactive as regards Louisiana. In the early
eighteenth century, about 1716, a Spanish
expedition moved eastward from Santa Fé
to check the French by establishing a military post in the upper Mississippi valley, but
it came to a disastrous end. So far as the
Louisiana territory is concerned the brilliant
beginnings of Spain suffered an inglorious
lapse. We owe to De Vaca, Coronado, and
De Soto the amplest knowledge which the
sixteenth century afforded of the interior of
North America, but the Spanish desire for
conquest and gold rather than real colonization and development proved impotent in
the end.

Many years later than the Spaniards—
not until the seventeenth century—came
the French, adventurous, impelled by pride
of country, desirous of territory and of trade,
but like the Spaniards lacking the colonizing
power of the race which finally dominated
Louisiana.

CHAPTER II

THE FRENCH IN LOUISIANA

Nicollet's early expeditions. Saint Lusson claims the West for France. Marquette and Joliet explore the upper Mississippi. La Salle descends to the mouth. The French claim to Louisiana. Tonty and other pioneers. The founders of New Orleans. The search for a way to the western ocean. Le Sueur and other explorers. The Verendryes see the Rocky Mountains.

It was nearly a century after the disastrous end of De Soto's journey and the return of Coronado's expedition before the first representative of the New France, which was pressing up the St. Lawrence, reached a tributary of the Mississippi. This was Jean Nicollet, a French interpreter of Three Rivers, whose journey westward as far as Green Bay and the Wisconsin River about 1634[1] was due to tales of a strange people, who, it was held, might be the Chinese. This Oriental myth, which

[1]As to the question of date see Winsor, Vol. IV, p. 304.

persisted so long, was not shattered by Nicollet's discovery that these "Orientals" were really Winnebago Indians. He returned believing that the Wisconsin River, which he claimed[1] to have reached and descended for a distance, had borne him within three days' journey of the sea.

Tales of the great river, the "Mesipi" of the Sioux, were brought back by adventurous French traders and priests in the years that followed Nicollet's quest. "Through what regions did it flow?" In Parkman's eloquent words, "Whither would it lead them,—to the South Sea or the Sea of Virginia, to Mexico, Japan or China? The problem was soon to be solved and the mystery revealed."

Of the gallant French explorers who first penetrated the interior of our country, one of the bravest and deservedly most famous was Robert Cavelier, born at Rouen in 1643 and

[1]C. W. Butterfield's "History of Discovery by Jean Nicollet," etc. (Cincinnati, 1881), indicates that Nicollet did not descend the Wisconsin. He was, however, the first white man to reach Green Bay.

best known as La Salle. At the age of twenty-
three he came to Canada. He became seignior
of an estate near Montreal, but ambition, love
of adventure, an ardor for discovery and conquest soon led
him to the ex-
ploration of the
unknown West.
It seems certain
that in 1669 he
journeyed from
Lake Erie to a
branch of the
Ohio and de-
scended at least
as far as the
falls at Louis-

LA SALLE

ville. But a more glorious journey or discovery was yet to come.

At nearly the same time Jean Talon,
intendant of Canada, was making the first
formal move in the great game which was
to checkmate England and Spain by a French
control of the interior that would confine

England to the eastern seaboard and hold the Spaniards at bay in the south and southwest. It was with this in view that in 1670 he ordered Daumont de Saint Lusson to Lake Superior to take possession of the interior. It was early in May that the French soldiers and priests assembled on a hill near the foot of the Sault Sainte Marie, surrounded by wondering Indians, who watched them raise a cross and place beside it a post bearing the arms of France. All the known country of the Great Lakes, all the contiguous countries discovered and undiscovered, "bounded on the one side by the seas of the North and of the West, and on the other by the South Sea," were claimed by Saint Lusson, sword in hand, as the possessions of "the most High, Mighty and Redoubted Monarch, Louis, Fourteenth of that name, Most Christian King of France and of Navarre."

Such was the proud claim of France covering the valley of the Mississippi and the country to the west; but of the geography of much of the western territory the French had little

more knowledge than the Spaniards in 1493
when the bull of Pope Alexander VI divided
the Western World between the Spaniards
and Portuguese.

Of the many
French soldiers,
priests, traders,
and adventurers
associated with
the early history
of the Louisiana
territory, the
most famous are
Father Mar-
quette and the
La Salle whom
we have met at
the outset of his
career. It was

LOUIS XIV, KING OF FRANCE

in 1673, sixty-five years after Samuel de
Champlain founded Quebec, that Louis Joliet,
an agent of Count Frontenac, governor of
New France, or Canada, and Father Marquette,
a Jesuit priest of singular devoutness and

unflinching courage, were commissioned to discover the great river which had proved so elusive,—the Mississippi. From Mackinaw they journeyed to Green Bay and entered Fox River. With the aid of Indian guides they found their way to a portage which brought them to the Wisconsin River. "They bade farewell to the waters that flowed to the St. Lawrence, and committed themselves to the current that was to bear them, they knew not whither,—perhaps to the Gulf of Mexico, perhaps to the South Sea, or the Gulf of California."[1]

AUTOGRAPH OF JOLLIET, OR JOLIET AS THE NAME IS USUALLY SPELLED

On June 17 they reached the present site of Prairie du Chien, Wisconsin, and there before them stretched the stream which was the object of their quest. Day after day, in spite of strange and terrifying adventures, they kept their way

[1]Parkman, "La Salle and the Discovery of the Great West."

FATHER MARQUETTE

(From Trentanove's statue in the Capitol at Washington)

This is an ideal figure. In 1897 a painting was discovered in Montreal which
is claimed to be a portrait.

down the great river, passing the mouth of the Missouri, which Lewis and Clark were afterwards to ascend, and finally reaching the mouth of the Arkansas. They were seven hundred miles from the mouth of the Mississippi, although they thought themselves much nearer; but their journey had made it clear that the Mississippi flowed southward to the Gulf of Mexico. This fact was ascertained, and, since below them lay danger from hostile Indians and possibly from Spaniards, they reëmbarked on July 17, and set forth on their arduous return journey to report their discovery. In accordance with the custom of these pioneer priests Father Marquette kept a careful journal, and this "Relation," as it is called, preserves the record of the perilous quest of a classic figure in the discovery of the West.[1]

In 1682 La Salle, seeking a trade route for the transportation of heavy skins, descended the Mississippi to its mouth. This was the first time that the entire course of the "Father of

[1]Mr. Reuben G. Thwaite's "Father Marquette" is an excellent presentation of this story.

Waters" had been traversed by a white man. On April 9, on the shore near the mouth, he

LA SALLE AT THE MOUTH OF THE MISSISSIPPI

erected a column bearing the arms of France and an inscription, and took possession of "this country of Louisiana" from "the mouth of the great river St. Louis, otherwise called the Ohio, . . . as also along the river Colbert,[1] or Mississippi, and the rivers which discharge themselves thereinto, from its source . . . as far as its mouth. . . ."

But after this triumph came a dangerous illness which kept him a prisoner at the Chickasaw Bluffs, while his faithful follower Tonty was dispatched to Michillimackinac[2] with tidings of his success. La Salle returned to France and was finally, in 1684, enabled to set sail for the

AUTOGRAPH OF TONTY

[1] A short-lived name given in honor of the minister of finance of Louis XIV.

[2] The name was applied generally by the French to the region about the Straits of Mackinac between Lake Huron and Lake Michigan. The island of Mackinac to the east was an early military post, and was also the first site of the mission of St. Ignace, afterwards transferred to the present site of St. Ignace on the mainland north of the straits, where Father Marquette was finally interred a year after his death in 1675 near the present site of Ludington, Michigan. A century later the English built a fort at the present site of Mackinaw City, south of the straits.

mouth of the Mississippi with a force which was to build fortifications, establish a colony, and hold the country against the Spanish. Through an error they landed at Matagorda Bay, in Texas, and there followed a squalid period of privation, suffering, and discontent, culminating in a conspiracy of La Salle's followers and the assassination of this brave explorer in 1687.

Several of those who served with La Salle made their mark in the early annals of the west. Joutel and Tonty, his loyal lieutenants, have left valuable records of adventurous explorations. Another less heroic figure was Father Hennepin, the discoverer of the Falls of St. Anthony at Minneapolis, who for a time accompanied La Salle. But Father Hennepin, unhappily, was romancer as well as historian.

To Pierre Le Sueur is due the credit of a journey in 1700 from the mouth of the Mississippi to the country of the Sioux, in the present state of Minnesota, and a return down the river. This journey was made in a profitless search for furs and mineral wealth. In the same year Pierre Le Moyne d'Iberville planned an expedition to the upper Missouri, lured by the hope of a western passage down some river to the western sea. In 1717 Hubert urged a similar plan upon the French Council of Marine.[1] The belief in the myth of the northwest passage[2] to the Orient was waning, but there was still faith, not wholly unfounded, in a nearly continuous river route to the western ocean, and, failing this, it was believed that a way could be made by land.

[1] In 1704 Bienville reported that over one hundred Canadians were scattered along the Mississippi and Missouri. In 1705 a Canadian named Laurain claimed to have ascended the Missouri, and in 1708 Nicolas de la Salle proposed a plan like those of Iberville and Hubert. In 1719 Du Tisné ascended the Missouri above Grand River. Afterward he crossed the state of Missouri and reached the Indians on the Osage River. The early eighteenth-century explorations of Saint Denis, La Harpe, Bourgmont, and the brothers Mallet, for the most part in the southern half of the Louisiana territory, in Texas, and even New Mexico, helped, in the language of Parkman ("A Half Century of Conflict"), "to unveil the remote southwest."

[2] This idea represented a phase of the long search for a northwest passage to the Orient, which is perhaps most closely identified in the popular mind with the early attempts in the region of Hudson Bay and in the Arctic.

Under the regency of the Duke of Orleans, in 1716, three posts were planned between Lake Superior and Lake Winnipeg to serve as bases of supplies for an overland expedition, and one was actually built at the mouth of the river Kaministiguia on the north shore of Lake Superior. But nothing more was done, and three years later Charlevoix, the Jesuit historian of early Canada, was ordered to visit the country and report upon a passage to the western sea. His report was that the Pacific probably lay just to the west of the country of the Sioux. One plan which he advocated was the ascent of the Missouri, "the source of which is certainly not far from the sea."

Iberville and Charlevoix had pointed to the Missouri as the route nearly a century before the journey of Lewis and Clark. Then came the Verendryes, who preceded the Americans almost to the Rocky Mountains.

La Verendrye the elder, a French soldier, explorer, and trader, built forts at the Lake of the Woods, on the site of Winnipeg, and at the mouth of the Saskatchewan. In the course

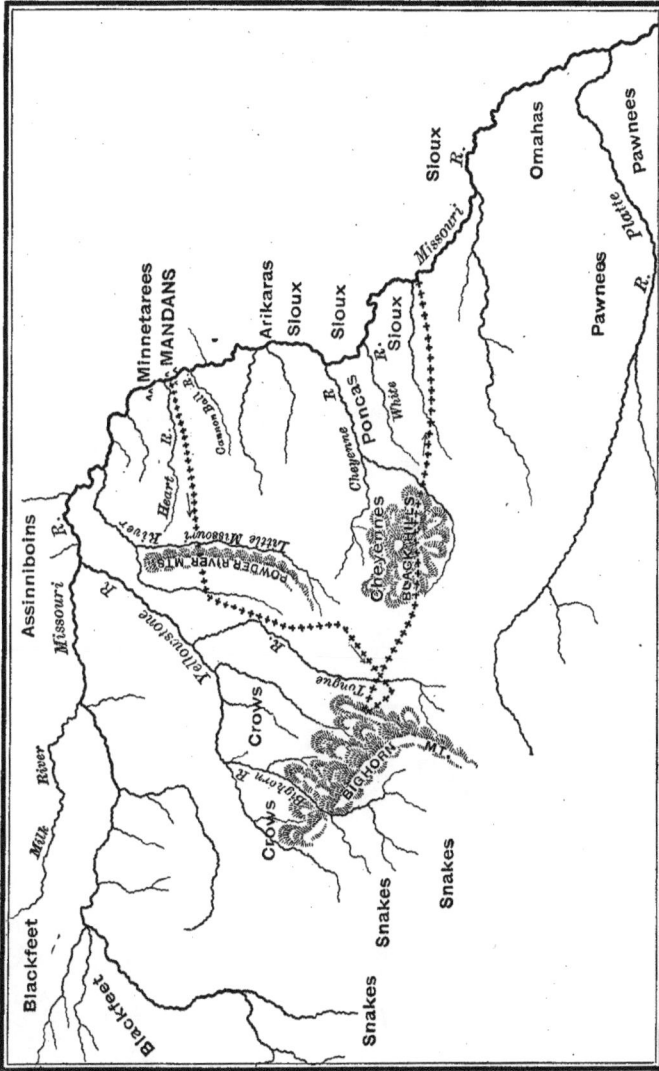

MAP OF THE VERENDRYES' ROUTE

of his expeditions he traveled as far as the Mandan villages on the Missouri in his search for the western sea. This was in 1738. It was among the descendants of these Mandans living near Bismarck, Dakota, that Lewis and Clark passed a winter nearly seventy years later.

In 1742 the two sons of Verendrye made their way to the Mandan villages, and undertook an expedition westward, under the guidance of the Indians, hoping to find the Pacific. They traveled between the Black Hills and the Missouri, entered Montana, and finally, after much uncertain journeying and many strange experiences with the nomadic tribes of Indians, the mountains rose before them. The Spaniards had crossed the mountains to the south, but the Verendryes were the first white men to see the true Rocky Mountains on the north. It was in January, 1743, that they discovered the mountains, probably the Big Horn range in Wyoming. In the records of French Louisiana the names of the Verendryes merit a place with those of Father Marquette and La Salle.

CHAPTER III

THE FRENCH IN THE EIGHTEENTH CENTURY

The founding of New Orleans. Extent of French possessions. The beginnings of St. Louis. The gateway of Louisiana. Downfall of French power. Louisiana ceded to Spain. American and English explorations. Oregon not included in Louisiana.

While French explorers and traders were following the northern rivers, signs of genuine colonization began to appear in the south. At the beginning of the eighteenth century three countries maintained conflicting claims to the valley of the Mississippi. Spain held Florida and based her claim to the westward on De Soto's discovery of the great river. France held the upper waters, and La Salle and others had descended the river to its mouth and asserted possession. The charters of some of the English colonies on the

34

seaboard embodied sweeping claims to territory from the Atlantic to the Pacific.

In spite of the doubts of King Louis XIV of France as to the value of the new country, he was finally persuaded to sanction the founding of a French colony at the mouth of the Mississippi. This was largely due to the enthusiasm of a gallant Canadian, Pierre

AUTOGRAPH OF LE MOYNE D'SIBERVILLE

Le Moyne d'Iberville, who sailed from France with an armed expedition in 1698. The first colony was established the year following at Biloxi, upon the Gulf of Mexico, within the present limits of Mississippi, but its checkered career was ended in 1718, when Bienville d'Iberville, a brother of Le Moyne, founded the city of New Orleans.

The early years of the French colonists were not prosperous. In an effort to make the colony a source of income rather than expense, the king in 1712 gave to Antoine Crozat an exclusive right to trade in that quarter. The failure of this plan resulted in its abandonment in 1717, and the Company of the West, better known as the Mississippi Company, was formed, which succeeded to Crozat's rights.

AUTOGRAPH OF BIENVIILE

Under the leadership of the notorious John Law, who for a time was a financial magnate in France, the company issued an unlimited amount of paper money without adequate security. This was done in part to further the interests of the company in the Mississippi

AUTOGRAPH OF JOHN LAW

valley; but after a period of wild excitement and speculation in France it was found that the paper money could not be exchanged for coin or solid property, and in 1721 there followed collapse, failure, and ruin. This was the end of what is known as the Mississippi Bubble.

In spite of the dismay and suffering caused by this failure, the growth of the colony was quickened during this era of speculation by enforced emigration from France, since it was

NEW ORLEANS IN 1719

necessary to settle and develop the new lands as quickly as possible. These troubles, with attacks by the Indians, illness, and lack of proper supplies, clouded the early years of French settlement in Louisiana; but the French remained, and later the colony began to enjoy prosperity.

Thus by discovery, exploration (and to some extent by colonization), and by the building of forts on the north and east, the French held the Mississippi valley, together with the vaguely known empire to the west. The word "colonization" must be accepted with limitations, for neither the French nor the Spanish were led by the motives which caused the English settlers to regard the new country as a permanent home and to develop it for the future as well as for the present. But while New Orleans was struggling through its early years at the mouth of the Mississippi, the French trappers and traders were descending the river from the north.

In 1762 M. d'Abbadie, the French director general of Louisiana, granted to Pierre Laclède, the head of a company of merchants, the exclusive right to trade with the Indians on the Missouri. Two years later this company founded the city of St. Louis, selecting its present site for the erection of a house and four stores. This was the beginning of the city, which for practically a century remained

the commercial center of the Louisiana territory. It was here that the American fur trade
had its headquarters, and up to nearly the
middle of the nineteenth century the traffic
in furs was the chief industry of the Louisiana
territory.[1] As time went on the commerce
of the Southwest and of the great river
passed in swelling volume
through St. Louis,
the gateway of the
West; but all this
was then in the
future. Even
before St. Louis
was founded a

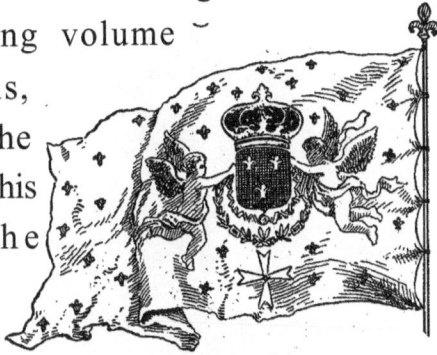

THE ROYAL FLAG OF FRANCE

change had come in the fortunes of France.
The long warfare between the French and
English in North America had culminated,
and the rule of France on this continent was
ended forever.

[1]The "History of the American Fur Trade," and the
"History of Early Steamboat Navigation on the Missouri
River," by Captain Hiram M. Chittenden, U.S.A., are indis-
pensable to students of the early nineteenth-century history
of the West.

In 1759 the English General Wolfe defeated the French General Montcalm on the Plains of Abraham, under the walls of Quebec. Four years later, in 1763, France ceded to England her American possessions east of the Mississippi, with the exception of New Orleans.[1] But New Orleans and the French possessions west of the Mississippi,—that is, the country of the Louisiana Purchase,—were secretly ceded to

MONTCALM

Spain by King Louis XV of France, who desired to cement a Spanish alliance.

In 1768 the first Spanish governor appeared at New Orleans, and northward from the sea

---

[1] In the same year Spain transferred Florida to England in exchange for Havana, but Spain received Florida back in 1783.

along the west bank of the Mississippi, fourteen hundred miles, the Spanish authority
prevailed. All the traffic down the Mississippi from the valley of the Ohio or elsewhere must pass under the Spanish flag.

The American Revolution was at this time
close at hand. Then there came the critical
period of the adoption of the Constitution and
the organization of the government of the
United States, so that the attention of the
American people was occupied elsewhere. For
nearly forty years the Spaniards, who had been
the first to penetrate the Louisiana Purchase,
held full possession, although, as we shall see,
France presently undertook to regain the country, and with the growth of the United States
west of the Alleghenies the American pressure
began to strain the arbitrary boundaries.

The Spaniards made no prolonged explorations to the north, but Americans and English
began to investigate the unknown and remote
west. Jonathan Carver, a native of New York
and an officer in the war with France, suggested an attempt to cross the northwest

portion of America by land. This was looked upon as visionary, but in 1766 Carver undertook an exploring expedition in which he followed the Minnesota River for some two hundred miles. The interest of this journey to us lies in the fact that Carver heard much from the Indians regarding the "Shining Mountains," as the Rocky Mountains were termed, and that he learned of the Oregon, or "River of the West," which is now the Columbia. It occurred to him that by ascending the Missouri it might be possible to cross to the head waters of the Columbia. But official indifference prevented the attempt. This idea was carried out nearly forty years afterward by Lewis and Clark. Twenty-five years later a Scotchman, Alexander Mackenzie, crossed the continent to the Pacific, but his route lay farther north, through what is now Manitoba and British Columbia.

On the Pacific coast the Spaniards held California, but they knew little of the Northwest. This was reached by the famous explorer, Captain Cook, who visited Alaska in

1778. Vancouver, another English explorer, sailed by the mouth of the Columbia without entering it; this was left for American enterprise. In 1787 some Boston merchants sent Captain Robert Gray in the sloop *Washington* and Captain John Kendrick in the ship *Columbia* around Cape Horn to the northwest coast to trade for furs, which were to be exchanged for silk and tea in China. So far as Gray was concerned the journey was successful, and after exchanging ships with Kendrick, Gray returned by way of China in the *Columbia,* which was the first ship to circumnavigate the globe under the American flag. On this first voyage Gray nearly lost his ship on the bar of an unknown stream, probably the Columbia. On his second voyage, in 1792, he entered and named the great river. His discovery was earlier than that of Vancouver and formed the basis of the subsequent claim to Oregon urged by the United States against Great Britain.[1] Gray was followed by other

[1]H. H. Bancroft argues for the discovery of the Columbia by Heceta in 1775, but Gray's discovery is generally

traders, and in a few years a regular trading post was established near the mouth of the Columbia.

While a knowledge of these northwestern explorations is desirable, it should be understood that Oregon, as the northwest beyond the Rocky Mountains was called, was not included in the Louisiana Purchase. The Louisiana Purchase extended only to the Rocky Mountains, but, as it was important to find a way across and to explore the Columbia to the sea, the task of finding a route to the Pacific was included in the instructions to Lewis and Clark.

accepted. The rival claims of Gray and Vancouver and their relation to the Oregon question are not essential here.

CHAPTER IV

THE AMERICAN WESTWARD MOVEMENT

Advancing beyond the Alleghenies. Settlement rather than exploration or exploitation. Experiences of the pioneers. Their way to the sea blocked by Spanish control of the mouth of the Mississippi. How the Spaniards ruled New Orleans.

After the long periods of desultory Spanish exploration, of French trading expeditions and attempts at military and commercial occupation which have been sketched in the preceding chapters, the history of Louisiana shows the influence of Americans bent upon actual settlement of the country to the westward of the Alleghenies.[1] The downfall of

[1] McMaster's "History of the People of the United States," Vol. II, and Roosevelt's "Winning of the West" give picturesque accounts of the pioneers and the significance of their movement. Hinsdale's "The Old Northwest," Winsor's "The Mississippi Basin (1697-1763)" and "The Westward Movement (1763-1798)" may be consulted with profit.

French power on this continent brought the beginning of another era in the history of Louisiana. But the operation of the forces represented in the American westward pressure was delayed, first by the Revolution, and then by the fierce opposition of the south-

GEORGE ROGERS CLARK

western and north-western Indian tribes who fought to hold the Middle West. In spite of all obstacles the way was opened by the rifles of the soldiers and frontiers-men who followed George Rogers Clark, Anthony Wayne, and other leaders in the winning of the West. Close behind them came a swelling tide of migration across the Alleghenies. The sound of the axes and rifles of the American pioneers along the eastern tributaries of the Mississippi marked the opening of a new epoch in the history of the West.

George Rogers Clark's Expedition to capture
Vincennes in 1779

Up to the end of the Revolution the possession of Louisiana territory by one foreign
power or another had
not touched Ameri-
cans closely. But
now the conditions
were changed. In
the western migra-
tion of the later
eighteenth century
and the demands of
these frontiersmen
for a free route to the

ANTHONY WAYNE

seaboard lay influences which finally resulted
in the acquisition of Louisiana.[1]

[1]"In 1784 Pittsburg numbered one hundred dwellings
and almost one thousand inhabitants. It was the centring
point of emigrants to the West, and from it the travellers
were carried in keel-boats, in Kentucky flat-boats, and Indian
pirogues down the waters of the Ohio, . . . to the filthy and
squalid settlements at the falls of the Ohio, or on to the
shores of the Mississippi, where La Clede, twenty years
earlier, had laid the foundations of St. Louis. . . . The boat
was at every moment likely to become entangled in the
branches of the trees that skirted the river, or be fired
into by the Indians who lurked in the woods. The cabin
was therefore low, . . . and lined with blankets and with

The growth of this movement is shown by the returns of the census for Kentucky, Tennessee, and the Northwest Territory, which then represented our West. In 1790 there were 73,677 people in Kentucky, and in 1800 there were 220,955. Tennessee showed 35,691 people in 1790, and 105,602 in 1800. The census of 1790 gives no population for Ohio and Indiana territories, but ten years later there were 44,678. Before these stalwart pioneers the forests were swept aside to make room for farms. Rude log cabins were built with chimneys of logs plastered with mud. The settlers made their simple furniture with their own tools. Their hunting shirts and trousers were of homemade linsey, a mixture of linen and wool, and of deerskin. Most of their food was gained by their rifles and their traps. Corn was pounded or ground in rude

beds to guard the inmates from Indian bullets. From St. Louis rude boats and rafts floated down the river to Natchez and New Orleans. . . . The current was so rapid that it seemed hopeless to attempt a return. The boats were therefore hastily put together and sold at New Orleans as lumber."—McMaster's History, Vol. I, pp. 69–70.

stone mortars to make meal. But the vigor
and energy of these hardy pioneers soon bet-
tered their condition. They began to raise
tobacco and wheat and to cure hams and
bacon. Then came the question of trade.[1]

How could they exchange these products
for money or for goods of which they stood in
need? There was no market at hand. The
railroad was yet in the future. To the eastward lay the Alleghenies and a long and
difficult journey by land impossible for their
purposes. Their easiest and cheapest route to
a market was by water, and close at hand
were the Ohio and other rivers flowing to the

[1]Certain economic phases of this pioneer life have been
summarized as follows: "Currency was very scarce and was
replaced by articles of general value, such as skins and jugs
of whiskey. Cowbells were also such a necessity that they
became an acceptable tender. Small currency was scarce,
and a silver dollar was often cut into half dollars or quarters
with an axe or chisel. . . . Salt was worth six cents a pound.
Beef sold at four cents a pound and deer meat at three. . . .
Corn was sold at fifty cents a bushel. A single log cabin
could be built for $150. Feather beds were a great luxury
and readily brought six dollars each. The family washing
was done on the river bank."—Sparks's "Expansion of
the American People."

Mississippi, and offering a tempting water way to New Orleans and the sea. But New Orleans was held by the Spaniards. Their laws and customs regulations were arbitrary;

A FLATBOAT ON THE OHIO

their business methods were antiquated, complicated, and irksome. Between their mediæval rule and the free and impatient spirit of the pioneers there was instant conflict. In the early nineties the Spanish authorities closed navigation and refused to grant the right to deposit goods at New Orleans to await the arrival of trading vessels. This right was essential for the men who journeyed down the great river in their "broad-horns," or rude homemade boats.

A crisis seemed at hand in 1795, but it was averted by the Spanish minister of state, Manuel Godoy, known as the "Prince of Peace,"[1] who more than once had proved his friendly feeling for the United States. In 1795 a treaty was signed, which granted the right of deposit, with certain minor limitations, for three years. Thus an outbreak was averted. The way to a market was kept open during the three years, and thereafter until 1802. Then the Spaniards withdrew the right of deposit, the West rose in protest, and therein lay a potent motive for the

[1]This remarkable title was derived from Godoy's negotiation of the treaty of Basel with France in 1795. His personal character was open to reproach, but in his attitude toward France and toward American interests at the mouth of the Mississippi he rendered valuable aid to the United States.

acquisition of at least the mouth of the Mississippi. But the immediate demand of these American settlers was not for Louisiana, but simply for an open seaport, or at most the possession of the river's mouth.

On the south, therefore, the Americans were shut in by Spain. In these days, when we have seen Spain losing the very last of her holdings in the Western Hemisphere, it is hard to realize the extent of her sway a little more than a century ago. A hundred years before our war with Spain the Spaniards held Texas, Mexico, and the Floridas, not to mention the West Indies and all of Central and South America except Brazil. They controlled the ports of Pensacola, Mobile, and New Orleans. The Spanish possessions ran from Fernandina to Natchez, and then north on the west bank of the Mississippi to the Lake of the Woods. Above New Orleans, as far as Point Coupée, there were plantations and villages. North of Point Coupée the west bank of the river was, with few exceptions, a wilderness.

The older part of New Orleans,[1] which was laid out under Bienville by the Sieur La Blonde de la Tour, was inclosed by ramparts. Most of the streets retained their French names. Outside the ramparts dwelt a motley colony of foreigners and Americans. Many of the latter were traders who had floated down the river in clumsy boats, bringing produce for sale or shipment. The levee was crowded with shipping and piled high with goods. Spanish officers, *regidores, alcaldes,* and *syndics,* ruled a city which offered a most picturesque mingling of Spanish, French, Creole, foreign, and American types. But while all this was undoubtedly picturesque, the mediæval customs of the Spaniards, and their many rules and taxes, were galling to the active and impatient Americans.

[1] McMaster, Vol. III, chap. xiv, gives a picturesque description of Spanish New Orleans.

CHAPTER V

LOUISIANA'S CRITICAL PERIOD

France tries to regain the West. Genet's intrigues. Attitude
of England and Spain. Napoleon's designs. Talleyrand's
plans for a colonial empire. Louisiana ceded to France.
Napoleon's plans checked by Toussaint's rebellion in San
Domingo.

If Spanish control of the outlet of our
western trade was bad, a French rule under
the aggressive Napoleon would have been
worse, and this began to appear as a possibility. The pride of the French had been
hurt by their cession of Louisiana to Spain.
So strong was this feeling that various efforts
were made by French ministers to regain the
lost territory. To the government of the
United States Louisiana became in the last
decade of the eighteenth century a source
of constant anxiety. From the beginning
of this decade to the consummation of the

54

purchase in 1803 was the most critical period in the varied history of Louisiana. Within our borders there was the expansion of a race not to be held in check. Without, the efforts of three great powers were concerned at various times with the possession of Louisiana. A mere outline of these efforts will illustrate the perils of the situation.

In 1790, when England and Spain were at variance, the English minister William Pitt contemplated a seizure of the Floridas and Louisiana, which Washington, and Jefferson, then secretary of state,

AUTOGRAPH OF GENET

rightly viewed as a menace to the future of the United States. Fortunately the danger passed, but only to be succeeded by a new peril.

France, eager to recover Louisiana, sent Genet as her minister to the United States in 1793 with a proposition for an alliance which should aim at the wresting of Canada from England and the seizure of Louisiana and the Floridas from Spain. When this "entangling foreign alliance" was declined, Genet, acting under secret instructions from his government, instigated movements in the Carolinas and Georgia to seize the Floridas, and in Kentucky to descend upon New Orleans. The frontiersmen were ready, but the progress of the French Revolution and the request of our government for Genet's recall prevented a frontier revolt against Spanish occupation which might have had results of lasting consequence.

The plottings of Genet to wrest Louisiana from Spain were followed by France's attempt to secure Louisiana through the treaty of Basel, which closed her war with Spain. In 1796, through the French minister to Spain, another effort was made in the series, which resulted in success in 1800. By 1797 there were added complications. The Spanish minister at Washington was expressing apprehensions of an invasion of upper Louisiana by the English. The English minister Liston denied the charge, but admitted that there had been some discussion of an invasion of Louisiana from the south. As a matter of fact, Senator Blount of Tennessee was implicated in this plot and was expelled from the Senate.[1]

In the following year Talleyrand broached his plan of a great colonial French empire in his formal proposition to Spain to exchange Louisiana for a principality to be made up of the papal legations and the duchy of Parma. This ambitious scheme was coupled with a generally in-imical attitude on the part of France, which

AUTOGRAPH OF TALLEYRAND

led to open hostilities on the sea between the United States and France in 1798–1799. England, stirred by the growing aggressive-ness of France, contemplated coöperation with the United States in the prevention of the transfer of Louisiana to France.

[1] The Spanish delay, 1795–1799, in removing troops from Walnut Hills, Chickasaw Bluff, and other river posts according to the treaty, irritated our West and influenced the Blount conspiracy.

Next, in 1800, came the secret treaty of retrocession by which Louisiana was to be returned to France, and in 1802 we find an English alliance again considered as a possible means of defense against French aggression.[1] In addition to these menaces of foreign interference we must bear in mind the pressure exercised at home by frontier settlers, sorely tried by Spanish exactions, and none too patient or law-abiding at the best. This pressure made the outcome inevitable.[2] The various parts which the question played in our own politics need not be dwelt upon in detail, but it contained possibilities not only

[1]"From the moment that France takes New Orleans we must marry ourselves to the British fleet and nation." —Jefferson to Livingston.

[2]"The winning of Louisiana was due to no one man, and least of all to any statesman or set of statesmen. It followed inevitably upon the great westward thrust of the settler folk, —a thrust which was delivered blindly, but which no rival race could parry until it was stopped by the ocean itself."

The fourth volume of Theodore Roosevelt's "Winning of the West," from which this extract was taken, was published in 1896, when the author could not foresee that the "westward thrust" of Americans was not to be stopped even by the ocean.

of most serious foreign embroilments but also of dangerous internal dissensions.

Of all these attempts upon Louisiana the most dangerous, and the most important as regards their unlooked-for outcome, were the efforts of France made through Talleyrand, who became minister of foreign affairs for the French Directory in 1797.

In the following year Talleyrand wrote the French minister at Madrid that the Floridas and Louisiana should be returned to France in order that the power of America might be bounded by the limits set by France and Spain. In 1800 Napoleon, then First Consul, endeavored again to secure Louisiana from Spain. When, on October 1, 1800, he signed the convention or agreement between France and the United States which closed the little war between the two countries, Napoleon at the same time drew up a secret treaty with Spain, providing that Louisiana should be given back to France. All knowledge of this was carefully kept from the world. Napoleon intended that nothing should be known of his plan until he was ready to land a force of troops at New Orleans. For this purpose the French portion of the island of San Domingo would be a most important base of operations.

But these plans were checked by a series of events which led even Napoleon to change his purpose. The influence of the Spanish minister Godoy kept King Carlos IV of Spain from signing the treaty with France until the autumn of 1802. In San Domingo there began in 1791 among the colored population an era of bloodshed which included civil war, massacre, and warfare against Spain and France, the powers which claimed control of the island. Out of this time of carnage and revolt rose the historic figure of Toussaint L'Ouverture.[1]

[1] "The story of Toussaint L'Ouverture has been told almost as often as that of Napoleon, but not in connection with the history of the United States, although Toussaint exercised on their history an influence as decisive as that of any European ruler. His fate placed him at a point where Bonaparte needed absolute control. San Domingo was the only center from which the measures needed for

One of the most curious of the many strange events associated with Louisiana is that Toussaint L'Ouverture, born a slave in the French part of San Domingo, should have done so much to thwart the ambition of Napoleon for a colonial empire. In 1794, after a period of civil war and anarchy in the island, the National Assembly of France abolished

AUTOGRAPH OF TOUSSAINT L'OUVERTURE

slavery, and the negroes, led by Toussaint, drove the Spaniards from the portion of the island which they held. He became the actual ruler, although San Domingo was nominally a colony of France. But he distrusted France and with reason, for Napoleon in spite of friendly

rebuilding the French colonial systems could radiate. Before Bonaparte could reach Louisiana he was obliged to crush the power of Toussaint."—"History of the United States," by Henry Adams, Vol. I, p. 378.

promises intended to crush the idea of freedom cherished by Toussaint and his followers.

When in 1798 the United States became
involved with France, and commercial relations were suspended, Toussaint declared his
independence and assured the United States
that he would safeguard trade if it were re-
newed. His soldiers coöperated with the
American fleet at the siege of Jacmel, a port
of San Domingo. But our half-war with
France came to an end. In Europe the
treaty of Amiens closed the war between
France and England, and then Napoleon was
free to crush Toussaint.

In 1802 Napoleon sent General Leclerc with
a great fleet and army to reconquer and occupy
the island. Although Toussaint had aided us
against France, the United States now made
no offer of intervention in his behalf. The
negroes fought desperately against the French,
but they were overmatched. Toussaint surrendered and was carried to France, where he
died in prison. There are grewsome pages
in the history of that insurrection, but

Toussaint's war for liberty will always touch the sympathies of American readers.

The victory of the French in San Domingo was dearly bought. Napoleon's purpose in the summer of 1802 was "to take possession of Louisiana in the shortest time possible." But Toussaint's rebellion and the ravages of yellow fever among the French troops involved delay and appalling loss. Time brought a change of purpose, and Napoleon's veterans never landed to occupy Louisiana and face the frontiersmen and soldiers of the United States.

CHAPTER VI

LOUISIANA AN ACTIVE ISSUE

The East slow to see the facts. Foresight of Washington, Jefferson, and Hamilton. A critical period. Spanish exactions. The river closed. Popular agitation. The West ready for war. Jefferson resolves to buy New Orleans and the Floridas. Monroe appointed commissioner. Livingston's work in Paris. Talleyrand's startling proposition. How Napoleon made his purpose known. A family quarrel in a bath-room.

Although the western expansion of Americans after the Revolution had made control of the Mississippi a question of swiftly increasing consequence, this had become apparent but slowly to the people of the East. A few statesmen saw the difficulties which were realized so forcibly by the pioneers who were pushing the frontier to the west. As early as 1782, while the negotiations were in progress which resulted in the establishment of peace with England by the Treaty of Paris the following year, Franklin wrote to Jay that to part with the Mississippi were as if one should sell his street door.[1] In 1790 Washington declared that "we must have and certainly shall have the full navigation of the Mississippi." It was a necessity pointed out in the same year by Jefferson when secretary of state. In 1799 Alexander Hamilton, even then in advance of his time, argued that we should possess not only the Floridas but the whole of Louisiana. Yet popular sentiment

ALEXANDER HAMILTON

in the East was slow to grasp the practical importance of an issue which became so acute

---

[1]The many complications with France and Spain as well as England which confronted the American Peace Commission are described in Winsor's "Narrative and Critical History," Vol. VII, chap. ii.

in the West as early as 1793 that Kentuck-
ians, as we have seen, advocated a resort to
force and were ready to follow the counsels
of Genet.

In the East the Mississippi question was
utilized by the Federalists in the first year of
the century as political capital. Their bitter
opposition to Jefferson, who became President
on March 4, 1801, led them to exult in the
dilemma which seemed forced upon him the
following year. On the one hand there was
an increasing possibility of war with France;
on the other, if the government failed to support the demands of the West and South, there
was a prospect of their secession and the dis-
solution of the Union. Jefferson's supporters,
the Republicans, argued for negotiation rather
than war. They pointed to the success of
Washington's diplomacy in averting another
war with England in 1794, and John Adams's
avoidance of a general war with France. It
was a situation in which an impetuous chief
executive might have precipitated a war.
Jefferson was emphatically a man of peace.

When Congress met in December, 1802, the President's annual message was awaited with intense eagerness; but it was absolutely pacific. This was not due to indifference. Jefferson had proved his interest in the West. It was in January, 1802, that his minister to France, Robert R. Livingston, learned of the secret treaty by which Spain retroceded Louisiana to France, a cession at first denied by Talleyrand. In May, Madison, Jefferson's secretary of state, was writing to Livingston regarding the menace of the cession,

LIVINGSTON'S AUTOGRAPH

and transmitting Jefferson's instructions for the acquisition from Spain of New Orleans and the territory east of the Mississippi in case the cession to France had not been accomplished.

In Paris Livingston followed closely the development of Napoleon's plans and labored to find a way of carrying out his instructions. In Washington Jefferson's peaceful and cautious policy influenced Congress at the outset to leave matters in his hands. But in the West and in the South peace was unknown. The news of the retrocession of Louisiana and the suspension of the right of deposit for American goods at New Orleans by the Spanish intendant, Morales, brought an outbreak which

JAMES MONROE

compelled recognition. Remonstrances and memorials were circulated through the West. State legislatures called for action. Troops were demanded to oppose the first attempt of the French to land at New Orleans. The West and the South clamored for freedom of trade, even at the cost of war.

It became inevitable that the government should take action. Jefferson appointed James Monroe as a special envoy to Paris with power to buy New Orleans and the Floridas for $2,000,000.[1] Here was the American beginning of the negotiations, which were intended to effect only the purchase of New Orleans and the Floridas.[2] It is true, however, that the

[1]JAN 11, 1803.

GENTLEMEN OF THE SENATE:
    . . . While my confidence in our minister plenipotentiary at Paris is entire & undiminished, I still think that these objects might be promoted by joining with him a person sent from here directly. . . .
    I therefore nominate Robert R. Livingston to be minister plenipotentiary, & James Monroe to be minister extraordinary & plenipotentiary, with full powers to both . . . or to either . . . to enter into a treaty or convention . . . for the purpose of enlarging & more effectually securing our rights & interests in the river Mississippi & in the territories eastward thereof. . . .   TH JEFFERSON
                (State Papers. For. Rel., Vol. II, p. 475.)

[2]It was not then known that France had acquired only Louisiana.

farsighted Livingston proposed that France should cede the Louisiana territory above the Arkansas River, but this was an idea of his own, and the instructions given by Jefferson were narrowly limited, as we have seen.[1]

The earnestness and ability with which Livingston labored in Paris to secure the Floridas and New Orleans and the free use of the Mississippi seemed to be poorly rewarded by the appointment of Monroe as a special commissioner to do practically what he was already trying to bring about. But the seriousness of the situation justified a special appointment, and it was Livingston after all who held the larger part in the negotiations. Meantime Livingston argued his case with Talleyrand, with Joseph Bonaparte, Napoleon's

[1]Jefferson's views at this stage are shown in a letter written to Monroe, January 13, 1803. "On the event of this mission depend the future destinies of the Republic. If we cannot by a purchase of the country, insure to ourselves a course of perpetual peace and friendship with all nations, then, as war cannot be far distant it behooves us to be immediately preparing for that course, without however hastening it; and it may be necessary, on your failure on the Continent, to cross the Channel."

brother, and with Barbé-Marbois, minister of the treasury. He boldly predicted a rupture with the United States in case France should occupy Louisiana and hold the mouth of the Mississippi and the Floridas.

For a long time his arguments seemed to carry little weight, but on April 11, 1803, Talleyrand met him with the startling proposition that the United States should buy the whole of Louisiana. This was not the plan of Jefferson; it was not the purpose of Livingston. Napoleon himself, in his usual arbitrary fashion, had changed his purpose and decided to offer the whole of the great Louisiana territory to the United States.[1]

---

[1]Disgust at the disastrous campaign in San Domingo, anger with Spain, a desire to be free for new campaigns in Europe, and a wish to be rid of the whole irritating subject of Louisiana are cited by Henry Adams as among the probable motives for Napoleon's change of mind. An essential motive was evidently due to the likelihood of a combination of England and the United States against France in case he occupied Louisiana. The result might well have been the exhaustion of France and the downfall of Napoleon long before Waterloo, with radical changes in European history and probably in our own.

Livingston's description of this remarkable event is quoted from a letter to Madison. "M. Talleyrand asked me this day when pressing the subject whether we wished to have the whole of Louisiana. I told him no; that our wishes extended only to New Orleans and the Floridas; that the policy of France, however, should dictate (as I had shown in an official note) to give us the country above the river Arkansas, in order to place a barrier between them and Canada. He said that if they gave New Orleans the rest would be of little value, and that he would wish to know 'what we would give for the whole.' I told him it was a subject I had not thought of, but that I supposed we should not object to twenty millions [francs,—about $4,000,000] provided our citizens were paid. He said this was too low an offer and he would be glad if I would reflect upon it and tell him to-morrow. I told him that as Mr. Monroe would be in town in two days, I would delay my further offer until I had the pleasure of introducing him."

NAPOLEON AS FIRST CONSUL

Leaving the American negotiations for a moment, it is worth while to go behind the scenes. First, Napoleon confided his purpose to Talleyrand, and later, on April 10, to Marbois and another of his ministers. The next day, a few hours before Talleyrand met Livingston, Napoleon summoned Marbois. In his usual peremptory fashion he exclaimed: "Irresolution and deliberation are no longer in season; I renounce Louisiana. It is not only New Orleans that I cede; it is the whole colony, without reserve. I know the price of what I abandon. I have proved the importance I attach to this province, since my first diplomatic act with Spain had the object of recovering it. I renounce it with the greatest regret; to attempt obstinately to retain it would be folly. I direct you to negotiate the affair. Have an interview this very day with Mr. Livingston."[1]

But it was Talleyrand, as we have seen, and not Marbois, who a few hours later startled Livingston with this unexpected change.

[1] For a full account of these negotiations see "History of the United States of America," by Henry Adams, Vol. II.

While the matter remained unsettled, there were not only the chances of discovery and opposition by Spain, and of irritation and change of plan on Napoleon's part, but there was also the pressure brought to bear by Napoleon's brothers, to prevent this sacrifice of French pride and possessions. His brothers Lucien and Joseph heard the news with astonishment and indignation. Summoning their courage they went to the Tuileries to protest, and were admitted to find the imperious ruler in his bath. Napoleon announced his purpose of selling Louisiana. "What do you think of it?" he asked Lucien. "I flatter myself," replied Lucien, "that the Chambers will not give their consent."

The First Consul retorted from his bath tub that he would do without their consent.

Joseph threatened to oppose him in the Chambers. He declared that they would all be punished by an indignant people. At this reply Napoleon lost his temper. "You are insolent!" he shouted, starting up, and then suddenly plunging back into his bath with a violence that sent the water flying into the faces of Lucien and Joseph. A servant who was present, frightened at the scene, fell fainting on the floor. Such was the stormy reception of Napoleon's decision in his own family. But he declared that his purpose was fixed in spite of the Constitution or the Chambers. And at the last Napoleon threatened Lucien, who lingered alone to maintain the argument, that if the latter undertook open opposition he would break him like the snuff-box which he hurled angrily upon the floor. And so the Napoleonic will prevailed.[1]

It has been said that the disregard of legal authority and of the wishes of the French people involved in this arbitrary decision marked a turning point in Napoleon's career. His act has been called a betrayal of his country. Yet after this he became the Emperor of France, and the most powerful single figure of his time.

---

[1] This amusing and yet serious bath-room scene is described in full in "Lucien Bonaparte et ses Mémoires," and summarized by Henry Adams, and by Dr. J. K. Hosmer in the latter's "History of the Louisiana Purchase."

CHAPTER VII

THE PURCHASE ARRANGED

Closing the bargain. The terms of payment. What was bought. Questions as to West Florida. The news in the United States. Federalist opposition. Debates over the right to buy and rule foreign territory. The treaty ratified. Provisions for government.

It was on April 11 that Livingston was surprised by Talleyrand's offer of the whole of Louisiana. The next day Livingston, recovering from his astonishment, endeavored to arrange the matter definitely, but the wily Talleyrand delayed lest he should cheapen the bargain by seeming too eager. Livingston was anxious to carry the affair as far as possible before Monroe took part.

After Monroe arrived, there followed a period of haggling over the price and terms. The price first mentioned on the French side was a hundred million francs ($20,000,000), with a provision that the United States should pay the claims of American citizens against France for depredations by French privateers, which amounted to twenty million francs ($4,000,000). Then Marbois, who presented this offer, dropped to eighty million francs ($16,000,000) for the territory and the claims. Finally, on April 29, the Americans agreed to Marbois's terms. The next day, April 30, their agreement was submitted to Napoleon. April 30 was adopted as the date of the treaty of cession and the convention regarding the payments, although the documents were not actually signed until a few days later.[1]

One curious feature of this checkered history is that the exact boundaries of the purchased territory were unknown. The treaty simply described the province of Louisiana "with the

[1]With this the work of the American negotiators was practically ended. Livingston resigned his post the next year and retired from public life; but the rest of his days were full of a usefulness which included his encouragement of Robert Fulton, the father of the steamboat. Monroe, continuing in public life, rose to the presidency of the United States.

same extent" that it had under Spain and earlier under France. The eastern boundary was
the Mississippi from its source to the parallel
of thirty-one degrees; but no one knew where
the source was, and the eastern boundary below
thirty-one degrees was in question, although
the Americans claimed the country as far as
the Perdido River.[1] The western boundary
was supposed to be the mountains, although
little was known regarding them; and the
northern limit was the ill-defined possessions
of Great Britain.

What was bought, therefore, was a vast ex-
panse of territory whose precise limits no one
knew. Again, the Floridas were not mentioned
in the treaty because they had not been ceded
by Spain, although the acquisition of West
Florida from the Mississippi to the river Perdido was part of the original American plan.
All that the commissioners obtained was
a verbal promise from Napoleon to use his
good offices with Spain in helping the United
States to gain West Florida. The Americans

[1]Now the boundary between Florida and Alabama.

claimed. West Florida as included in the sale under the French title. The claim was denied by Spain, but in 1810 a successful local revolution against Spain resulted in the formal annexation of West Florida to the United States.

The exact cost of the Louisiana territory was sixty-four million francs, in the form of United States six per cent bonds, representing a capital of $11,250,000.[1] In addition to this the American government agreed to assume and pay the obligations of France to American citizens for French attacks upon American shipping. These were estimated at twenty million francs, or $3,750,000, making the total payment $15,000,000. Troubles and scandals arose from the settlement of these claims, but that forms no part of this history.

With the money paid for the Louisiana territory Napoleon had intended to construct a system of canals; but war broke out almost

[1]The ultimate cost would include not only the par value of the bonds but also ten years' interest and the costs of surveying, of government explorations, and of selling lands, etc.

immediately, and by another of the curious turns of fate which accompanied the whole affair, this money was spent by Napoleon in preparations for an invasion of England which never took place.

President Jefferson had hoped to secure New Orleans and West Florida at a cost of not more than $2,000,000. But there came from Paris the astonishing tidings that the commissioners had bought the whole Louisiana territory and had agreed to pay $15,000,-000. The great news was promptly seized upon by the politicians and the people. The party opposed to Jefferson, the Federalists, attacked the purchase. They ridiculed the vague stories told of the unknown interior, and condemned the acquisition of a wilderness; but by the majority of the people the purchase was approved. Nevertheless, there were new and serious questions to be settled concerning the rights and powers of the United States as regarded the acquisition of foreign territory and its government. They were questions not unlike those discussed when the

United States, after the late war with Spain, acquired the Philippines and Porto Rico.

THOMAS JEFFERSON

In October, 1803, Congress met. Jefferson himself was a strict constructionist of the Constitution, and believed in states rights. He held that Congress had only such powers as were definitely delegated to it and such as were necessary to carry out the delegated powers. He believed that this treaty providing for the incorporation of foreign territory was in violation of the Constitution. He held at first that an amendment to the Constitution would be necessary before action could be taken upon the treaty. But he was confronted with a practical issue of grave and immediate moment. Statesmen holding views as extreme as his own argued for the constitutionality of the acquisition. Jefferson yielded his opinions to the practical exigencies of the situation, believing, as was the case, that the popular view would approve his course. Federalists, as well as Republicans, agreed that the United States could acquire territory.[1]

As to the status of the inhabitants of the Louisiana territory, another question was

[1] Later the right to annex territory was upheld by the Supreme Court. Professor McLaughlin, "History of the American Nation," p. 264, cites the case of Am. Ins. Co. *v.* Canter, 1 Peters, 511.

presented which was seized upon by the Federalists. The treaty contemplated their early admission to the rights of citizens of the United States,—Louisiana was not to be a dependent colony, without a vote or the prospect of statehood. This was bitterly opposed by the Federalists. It was argued that the vote of each individual state was necessary for the admission of a new state. The New England Federalists, foreseeing a lessening of their power through the admission of southern and western states, were strenuous antagonists of the measure. In some cases there was talk of secession.

Again the treaty gave special privileges to the vessels of France and Spain at New Orleans, although the Constitution required that duties should be uniform. This was defended by the claim that "Louisiana is purchased by the United States in their federal capacity, and is in the nature of a colony whose commerce may be regulated without reference to the Constitution." The far-reaching importance of these arguments,

and of the precedent established by the ratification of the treaty, has been illustrated in
the discussions over the recent acquisition of
Porto Rico and the Philippines.[1] The discussion of these questions was long and bitter, but
the treaty was ratified October 19, 1803.

After the treaty was ratified and the bill to
provide payment for the purchase was passed
still another question arose,—How should the
territory be governed? In spite of Federalist
opposition it was voted that until Congress
should provide a temporary government all
the military, civil, and judicial powers should
be exercised by persons to be appointed by the
President, without the advice or consent of

[1]"This broad interpretation of the treaty-making power
by the strict constructionist and state rights party itself,
paved the way for an imperial expansion of the United
States. Not only that,—it laid the foundations for a
readjustment of sectional power within the Union."—
Professor Frederick J. Turner, in the *Review of Reviews*
(May, 1903). This article, which has been consulted in
the preparation of this chapter, in addition to Adams,
McMaster, and others, is a remarkably clear and concise
presentation of political and constitutional phases of the
purchase.

the Senate. This act was approved by the President on October 31, 1803. It was a temporary measure intended to apply to the taking possession of the new country rather than to its permanent occupation. The formal act of taking over Louisiana was the next step in this eventful history.

CHAPTER VIII

TRANSFER TO THE UNITED STATES

Louisiana still in Spain's hands. Delivery to France. Cession by France to the United States. A country without government. Congress gives the President power. Importance of the precedents. The territory divided. A last foreign invasion.

Another curious feature of this history is that although France had sold Louisiana to the United States, it had not yet been delivered by Spain to France. On the 30th of November, 1803, however, this ceremony was formally performed in the old *Cabildo* (City Hall) of New Orleans. The French commissioner, Laussat, delivered to the Spanish commissioners the order of the king of Spain for the transfer of the province to France, and showed the authority which Napoleon had given him to receive it. Then the Spaniards yielded the keys of New Orleans and absolved the people from

86

allegiance to Spain. The Spanish flag was low-
ered, the French tricolor rose in its place, and
the reign of Spain in Louisiana was ended.

The next step was the formal cession to
the United States, and there were reasons for
haste. Spain had protested against the act of
France in selling the territory, for there was
a clause in the original treaty which forbade
its alienation.[1] These protests were so strong

[1] An interesting modern Spanish view of the Louisiana
Purchase has been afforded by Señor Jeronimo Becker,
archivist of the ministry of state, in *La España Moderna* for
May, 1903. This writer maintains that after securing the
cession of Louisiana back to France, Talleyrand assured the
Spanish government that the cession was desired merely for
display and effect, and that later, on the payment of two
million dollars, half in cash, Louisiana would be returned
to Spain.

Señor Becker also states that in 1815 the Spanish government hoped to regain Louisiana through the action of the
Congress of Vienna, and Labrador, the Spanish representative, was instructed to make the attempt. He saw that this
was impossible, but it was believed in Vienna in 1815 that
the English were in possession of New Orleans and therefore
practically of Louisiana, and he suggested that they might
be willing to transfer it to Spain,—a plan, he added, which
was approved by the Duke of Wellington. Señor Becker
expresses a feeling of inherited resentment against France
on account of the sharp practice by which Napoleon obtained

that Jefferson even prepared to meet an armed resistance by sending a small military force under General James Wilkinson[1] to New Orleans. Furthermore, in this interval there was no formal government in that city.

Jefferson appointed William C. C. Claiborne, governor of Mississippi territory, and General Wilkinson as the American commissioners to receive Louisiana. On December 20 they were

WILKINSON'S AUTOGRAPH

escorted into the city by American troops and were received by Laussat in the *Cabildo*. The ceremonies performed at the Spanish cession twenty days before were repeated now for the

Louisiana from Spain in exchange for the award to the Duke of Parma of the so-called kingdom of Etruria, which remained under the control of French soldiers after Napoleon had sold Louisiana to the Americans and the Americans were claiming the Floridas. But he shows no ill-will at the action of the United States.

[1] An unfortunate representative of the United States. His apparent willingness to prove false to his country in connection with Burr's plottings, and his military incompetency, have not been palliated by his acquittals.

The Cabildo, or City Hall

Copyright, 1906, by Detroit Photographic Company

most part, with one vital difference. This time the flag of France was replaced with the Stars and Stripes. It was the outward sign of a new destiny, the beginning of a new life richer and greater than any one who watched the unfurling of the flag could have dared to imagine.

Claiborne assured the people that their liberty, property, and religion were safe, and that they should never again be transferred. His assurance must have meant little to his hearers, in view of the many changes of the past.

CLAIBORNE'S AUTOGRAPH

"Ninety-one years before," says Professor Mc-Master, "when scarcely a thousand white men dwelt on her soil, Louis XIV had farmed Louisiana to Antoine Crozat, the merchant monopolist of his day. Crozat, unable to use it, made it over in 1717 to John Law, director-general of the Mississippi Company, which surrendered it in 1731 to Louis XV, who gave it in 1762 to the king of Spain, who made it over to Napoleon, who sold it to the United States." No wonder a promise that there would be no more changes was received with doubt. Yet, except for a short interval of fifteen months in the course of the Civil War, the Stars and Stripes have continued to wave over New Orleans.

For a short time Louisiana, although American territory, was without American laws or custom-house regulations. The merchants found themselves continuing to pay the obnoxious duties exacted by the laws of Spain, and they were not slow to protest. But early in 1804 Congress took action. After much discussion a law was passed dividing the purchased country at the thirty-third parallel, which afterward became the dividing line between Arkansas and Louisiana. The country north of that line was called the district of Louisiana, and was placed under the territorial government of the Indiana territory. There were but few white people then in this great stretch of country, but lower Louisiana, which was called the territory of Orleans, contained some fifty thousand people, or more than the territory of Ohio in 1800.

It was provided that the territory of Orleans was to be governed by officers appointed by the President. This was a step of great historical importance. First, the President had bought a foreign colony without its consent and had annexed it. Secondly, he assumed control of its government, and in both measures he was sustained by Congress. This was done without any changes in the Constitution. Another striking feature was that, although the treaty with France provided for full citizenship for the people of the Louisiana territory, this was denied them, and a government was established which was not elected by themselves but appointed from Washington. However, in spite of the surprises, the contradictions and compromises which accompanied the strange history of Louisiana, it became and it has remained American territory.

Only once, since it passed into our keeping, has Louisiana been threatened by a foreign invader. This was in 1815, at the end of our

war with England. But Sir Edward Paken-
ham's army of twenty thousand veteran British
soldiers, who came to conquer Louisiana, was

ANDREW JACKSON RIDING ALONG THE LINES AFTER THE
BATTLE OF NEW ORLEANS

defeated by the forces led by Andrew Jackson
in the battle of New Orleans, January 8, 1815.
As if to continue the list of strange events
which have been connected with Louisiana, this

battle was fought after peace had been arranged between the United States and Great Britain.

Two other events in our domestic history have menaced the integrity of Louisiana. Associated with the pacific Jefferson as Vice President was the brilliant, unscrupulous, and tragic figure of Aaron Burr. Burr's connection with the President who acquired Louisiana added another dramatic element to the history of plots which involved the West. As to the exact nature of Burr's schemes or conspiracy in 1805–1806, students have differed. The usual belief has been that Burr, spurred by diseased ambition and wounded vanity, planned the separation of the Southwest from the United States and the foundation of an empire under his own rule.[1] Later researches[2] go to indicate that Burr proposed to organize a filibustering expedition for the invasion and occupation of the Spanish territory to the

[1]See "History of the United States of America," by Henry Adams, for the argument that Burr proposed both treason to his country and filibustering.

[2]See "The Aaron Burr Conspiracy," by Dr. W. F. McCaleb.

south. At the outset, at least, Burr's designs were probably little better than treason, although his final purpose seems to have changed. Another figure in the history of Louisiana, Wilkinson, who was governor of New Orleans, was implicated in Burr's plots and sought to clear himself at Burr's expense.

While this plot, however, left the Louisiana Purchase unchanged, our Civil War made an inroad, fortunately only temporary, upon its integrity. In the fateful spring of 1861 the states of Louisiana and Arkansas seceded from the Union and joined the Confederacy. But in 1868 the constitutional relations of these states to the Union were fully reëstablished, and since then there has been and is likely to be no break in the relation of Louisiana to the United States.

LOUISIANA

═══════

PART II

THE LEWIS AND CLARK EXPEDITION

CHAPTER IX

EXPLORING LOUISIANA

An unknown interior. Jefferson's early interest in exploration. Ledyard's vain attempt. Jefferson selects Lewis and Clark. Who they were. Their instructions. The uncertainty as to their route.

The little that had been learned by 1803 of the interior of Louisiana came for the most part from the stories of Indians and of trappers. There were tales of vast prairies far in the interior, covered with herds of buffalo, and clothed with grass "because the soil was far too rich for the growth of trees." In the north, as Jefferson reported to Congress, there were great bluffs which were "faced with lime and free stone, carved into various shapes and figures by the hand of nature, and [they] afford the appearance of a multitude of antique towers." While this report was true, since it referred to the strange rock forms of the Bad

Lands of Dakota, it was laughed at by Jefferson's opponents.

Another story that Jefferson gravely repeated to Congress was of a wonderful mountain of

BAD LANDS OF DAKOTA

salt some thousand miles up the Missouri. It was said that this mountain was one hundred and eighty miles long and forty-five miles wide; that there were no trees or shrubs on it, but that it was one huge mass of glittering white. If any one doubted this fabulous tale, he was assured that samples of the salt had been shown at St. Louis. Even this failed to convince Jefferson's opponents, the Federalists. One newspaper writer suggested that the salt mountain was Lot's wife. Another writer imagined a salt eagle on the top and a salt mammoth climbing up the side. There were other stories of giant Indians as mythical as the salt mountain. From these strange reports one can realize how little was known of a part of our country which is now so familiar.

We have seen that Jefferson did not intend to buy the whole Louisiana territory, but he proposed an exploration of the West long before the purchase was made. In 1785 he was appointed minister to France, and in Paris he met John Ledyard, an American traveler. Ledyard had accompanied the famous navigator, Captain Cook, on his last voyage, when Cook sailed up the western coast of North America toward Bering Strait, and then sailed south to Hawaii, where he was slain by the natives. Ledyard was eager to continue his travels, and Jefferson proposed that he should cross northern Europe and Asia to Kamchatka, sail over to the present Alaska, and then go south "to the latitude of the Missouri and penetrate to and through that to the United States." Jefferson's language shows how uncertain the knowledge of the time was. No one knew where the Missouri River began. Ledyard undertook this adventurous journey, and on his overland route actually arrived within two hundred miles of Kamchatka; but there he was arrested by Russian soldiers and forced to return. This was the end of a plan which might have added a wonderful chapter to the history of American exploration.

But Jefferson's zealous desire for a knowledge of the West continued unabated. In 1792 he proposed to the American Philosophical Society to raise money for an exploration of the West. He suggested that some one should do this by "ascending the Missouri, crossing the Stony [Rocky] Mountains, and descending the nearest river to the Pacific." This suggestion brought a prompt application from Captain Meriwether Lewis, of the United States army, who was eager to make the journey. But Captain Lewis's time had not yet come.

MERIWETHER LEWIS

(From a print in the *Analectic Magazine* (1815) reproducing the drawing
by St. Merain, which belonged to Captain Clark)

The offer of André Michaux, a French botanist, was accepted, and he actually started on his journey. But when he had reached Kentucky on his way west he was overtaken by an order from the French minister, directing him to return and engage in other work. Thus Jefferson's second attempt at the exploration of the Louisiana territory also resulted in failure.

But the proverbial third attempt succeeded brilliantly. Before the Louisiana territory had actually passed into our hands Jefferson and others felt that it was quite time to learn more definitely what this strange country contained. In January, 1803, he seized the opportunity offered by the need of regulating trade with the Indians, to send a confidential message to Congress, in which he advised an exploration. Congress approved, and an appropriation of money was made. President Jefferson selected Captain Lewis as leader of the expedition and associated with him Captain William Clark.[1]

[1]Meriwether Lewis was born near Charlottesville, Virginia, in 1774. At eighteen he was a farmer. In 1794 he

There were, therefore, two leaders, but they did their memorable work without jealousy or trouble. Both were men of courage and resolution, fully equipped by character and training for the work which lay before them. Lewis possessed a rare power of discipline and executive ability, and a considerable scientific knowledge. Clark was peculiarly familiar with Indian habits, and his military training had borne good fruits.

served in the militia during the "whisky insurrection," and later obtained a commission in the regular army. Between 1801 and 1803 he was the private secretary of President Jefferson. In 1806 he was made governor of Missouri territory. He died in 1809.

William Clark, also a Virginian, was born in 1770, the brother of General George Rogers Clark who conquered the old Northwest for the United States in the Revolutionary War. In the boyhood of William Clark his family removed to Kentucky, then "the dark and bloody ground," as it was called from the frequent attacks of the Indians. With such an early experience it was not strange that Clark should become a soldier. But in 1796 he resigned from the army on account of ill health. He took up his residence in St. Louis, where he lived until President Jefferson offered him, in 1803, a military appointment as second lieutenant in the regular army and the joint command of the expedition. The title of captain came from his former rank in the militia of the Northwest.

Among the careful instructions given to Lewis and Clark we find that they were "to explore the Missouri River and such principal streams of it, as by its course and communication with the waters of the Pacific Ocean, whether the Columbia, Oregon, Colorado, or any other river, may offer the most direct and practicable water-communication across the continent, for the purposes of commerce." Since the Missouri rises east of the Rocky Mountains, the Colorado far to the southward, and the Columbia flows to the Pacific on the western side of the mountains, Jefferson's words illustrate the vague knowledge of the time.

The explorers were to take frequent observations of latitude and longitude and to note the courses of the river, points of portage, and all important features. Several copies of these observations were to be made. The thoughtful Jefferson recommended that one copy be on "the cuticular membrane of the paper-birch, as less liable to injury from damp than common paper."

Every feature of Indian life was to be studied with the greatest care. The explorers were to note the soil and face of the country, its vegetable products, its animals, the remains of any animals "which may be deemed dead or extinct,"[1] the mineral productions of every kind, volcanic appearances, and climate. They were to investigate the opportunities for trade and cultivate the friendship of the Indians. On the Pacific coast they were to see whether the fur trade of the far Northwest could not be conducted through the Missouri and the United States instead of by circumnavigation from Nootka Sound on the Pacific coast.

Clearly, the explorers had plenty of work laid out for them. How uncertain the outcome was in Jefferson's mind is shown by his directions that they should return from Oregon by sea, "by the way either of Cape Horn or the Cape of Good Hope," in case the return overland seemed "imminently dangerous."

[1]This is peculiarly interesting in view of the wonderful fossil remains found of late years in the Bad Lands of Dakota and elsewhere in the Northwest.

Furthermore, he said, the American consuls at
Batavia in Java, in the Isle of France, and at
the Cape of Good Hope would furnish money.
When we think of the present ease and luxury
of travel across the continent to Oregon it is
hard to realize that these doubts and difficulties existed only a hundred years ago.

CHAPTER X

PREPARING FOR THE JOURNEY

An uninformed Spaniard. A company of picked men. Some curious supplies. The journal of the expedition.

On July 5, 1803, Captain Lewis left Washington for Pittsburg. With Captain Clark he gathered stores and recruited his men from the military stations along the Ohio River. All this took time. It was not until December that they reached St. Louis. They intended to pass the winter at La Charrette, the uppermost settlement on the Missouri. But this was still held by the Spaniards. Although Louisiana by this time had passed from Spain to France and from France to the United States, the Spanish commandant had not yet been officially notified. At that day, when railroads were unknown, it required a month and a half for letters from eastern cities to reach St. Louis. The commandant refused to allow this armed force to enter Spanish territory. Lewis and Clark therefore recrossed the Mississippi to the eastern or American side, and passed the winter of 1803–1804 at

WASHINGTON ONE HUNDRED YEARS AGO

the mouth of Wood River, a little above St. Louis. While they are waiting there we may inspect their force and their equipment for the great journey which lay before them.

Picked men were needed for such perilous work. They were chosen wisely with a view to their special fitness for the task. There were fourteen soldiers selected from a large number who had volunteered from the regular army. There were nine young frontiersmen from Kentucky, men who had used the rifle from boyhood in hunting and in Indian warfare. There were two French canoemen, or *voyageurs,* one of whom could speak many Indian languages, while the other was a skilled hunter. These men were all enrolled as privates in the army, and with a negro servant of Captain Clark they made up the force. Three of the men were appointed sergeants. In addition, a corporal and six soldiers with nine boatmen were sent to accompany the expedition until they should reach the Mandan Indians, who dwelt near the present site of Bismarck, North Dakota. It was a small force, but a large company would have had difficulties over supplies, and would have excited the suspicions and hostility of the Indians.

The first necessities were food, clothing, tools, the flintlock rifles of the time, and a supply of powder, ball, and flints. But it was

French Fort at Saint Louis

necessary also to provide for the Indians who might be encountered. In order to make friends of them there were fourteen bales and one box of gold-laced coats, medals, flags, knives and tomahawks, beads, looking-glasses, and paints, which were to be given as presents. The expedition's own stores were contained in seven bales and a box.

For transportation there was first a keel boat fifty-five feet long and drawing three feet of water. This was decked over at bow and stern, thus forming a forecastle and a cabin. The middle was covered with lockers, which could be raised to form breastworks in case of attack. This boat had one large sail and twenty-two oars. There were two other boats, both open, one with six and one with seven oars. Two horses were to be led along the banks for the use of the hunters.

One of the strange turns of fate which appear so often in the history of Louisiana awaited the records of this expedition. The journals of the explorers were kept most carefully. President Jefferson used some of this material in his messages to Congress, and his citations were republished under a false claim that they gave the complete narrative. The actual journals were revised and largely re-written by Nicholas Biddle of Philadelphia, but it so happened that another was able to claim the editorship, and they were published in 1814 with the name of Paul Allen on the title-page as editor. This Biddle edition was republished in several foreign countries. The story of the Lewis and Clark expedition, as told in this volume, is taken from the Biddle text.[1]

[1]There have been many different editions, ranging from the elaborate and carefully annotated edition of Dr. Elliott Coues, to inexpensive small reprints. An abridged edition was published at New York in 1842 and reprinted several times. Mention should be made of William R. Lighton's excellent "Lewis and Clark," and the useful condensed narrative prepared by the late Noah Brooks in 1901.

But with all this array of editions it has so happened that the revised Biddle text has always been followed. The original journals have not been reprinted as the explorers wrote them, although Mr. Reuben G. Thwaites is now engaged in preparing them for publication.

CHAPTER XI

STARTING FOR THE WILDERNESS

Trappers and Indians. Across Missouri. The first sight of buffalo. Turning northward. A council with the Indians near Council Bluffs. An odd way of fishing. A country full of game.

On May 14, 1804, the travelers left their camp at the mouth of the Wood (now the Du Bois) River near St. Louis.

The route before them was up the Missouri and the Yellowstone on the eastern side of the Rocky Mountains, over the mountains and down Lewis's River (now known as Salmon River), the Clearwater, and the Columbia on the western side. The country which they were to pass through has since been divided into Missouri, Kansas, Iowa, Nebraska, South Dakota, North Dakota, Idaho, Washington, and Oregon. The total length of the journey was to be some eight thousand miles.

It was to last from May, 1804, to September, 1806. From April, 1805, to August, 1806, they were to be wholly shut off from the civilized world.

It was not until four o'clock in the afternoon of the 14th that they finished their packing and pushed off their boats, and they had made only four miles when night forced them to land for the first camp of the journey near Cold Water Creek, just above Bellefontaine.

At St. Charles, which bears the same name to-day, they were overtaken on May 21 by Captain Lewis, who had been detained at St. Louis, and that afternoon they started on in the face of wind and rain.

A few days later they met some canoes laden with furs obtained among the "Mahar," or Omaha, Indians. These meetings are of interest because the trappers and the fur traders were the real pioneers of the far West. Their work was the chief industry of that great region for the first forty years of the last century.

On June 1 the expedition camped at the mouth of the Osage River, named from the

Osage Indians. The Dakotan name of these Indians was the Wabashas, from which comes the name Wabash. They believed themselves descended from a snail and a beaver, and for a long time they held the beaver sacred. But the demand for furs proved stronger than the tradition, and in spite of relationship the beavers suffered from the fur hunters.

Another camp was made at Moreau Creek, a little below the present Jefferson City. French fur traders were met, and at Little Manitou Creek (now Moniteau Creek in Missouri geographies) the explorers saw a strange figure resembling "the bust of a man with the horns of a stag," which had been painted by the Indians on a projecting rock.

As they went on they entered the country of the Ayauway Indians, which was one of the many ways of spelling Iowas. Here they found deer and bears, and one of the hunters brought in a remarkable story of a small lake where "he heard a snake making a guttural noise like a turkey." The venison which the hunters obtained was frequently "jerked" for preservation; that is, it was cut into ribbons and dried in the sun.

The expedition had now advanced some two hundred and sixty miles up the Missouri, to a point between Saline and Carroll counties, which lies not far from the center of the state of Missouri. Continuing a journey which for the time was comparatively uneventful, they crossed the state of Missouri on their steady way up the river, and on June 26 they reached the mouth of the Kansas River, which flows easterly through the state of Kansas. Here they found a village of Kansas Indians, most of whom were away on the plains "hunting for buffalo, which our hunters have seen for the first time."

This home of buffalo hunters at the mouth of the Kansas River has now given place to Kansas City, Missouri, and Kansas City, Kansas.

At this point the Missouri turns northwesterly on the ascent, and the explorers were on a straighter course to their destination. On the left, ascending, are now the Kansas counties of Leavenworth, Atchison, and Doniphan,

and on the right the Missouri counties of
Platte, Buchanan, Andrew, and Holt; while
above Kansas City they passed the sites of
the future cities of Leavenworth, Atchison,
and St. Joseph. Nearly all the points mentioned in their narrative have been identified,

IN THE DAYS OF THE BUFFALO HUNTER

but it will be more interesting to follow the
story of their adventures than to go far into
geographical details.

By the middle of July they had reached
Nebraska and Iowa. The hunters found deer
and wild geese, one boat was nearly wrecked
on a sand bar in a storm, and there was some

illness which was thought to be due to their drinking the muddy river water. On July 21 they reached the mouth of the great Platte River, where at night many wolves were seen and heard.

Some ten miles above the Platte River the explorers camped on the east side of the Missouri, probably about ten miles below the present cities of Council Bluffs and Omaha. There they dried their provisions and prepared letters to be sent to the President when the chance came. The hunters saw deer and turkeys; there were many wild grapes, and one man caught a white catfish.

Messengers were sent to ask the Pawnee Indians to visit them, but the Indians were away hunting the buffalo. A few days later, however, after the explorers had advanced further northward, they succeeded in reaching them, and their first formal council with them was held on August 3. Some fourteen Ottoe (or Otto) and Missouri Indians were assembled under an awning formed of the mainsail. They were informed that the United States

now ruled the country and promised them pro-
tection. The chiefs expressed their joy and
asked to be commended to the Great Father
(the President). They requested that arms be
given them and that they be protected from
their enemies, the Omahas, which was promised. Then followed a distribution of presents,
medals, paint, garters, and cloth ornaments,
with a canister of powder and a bottle of
whisky,—the last certainly an unfortunate
gift. Then the explorers fired their air gun,
which astonished the Indians greatly, and this
ended the ceremonies of the first council.

The name of the city of Council Bluffs comes
from this meeting, but the actual council was
held on the west side of the river and several
miles above the city.

A few days later the travelers saw a large
mound with a pole fixed in the center, on a
sandstone bluff, and learned that it was the
grave of a chief named Blackbird, who died
of smallpox, from which the tribe had suffered seriously. Blackbird was described by
another traveler as a chief whose fame was

due largely to the fact that he had obtained from a trader some arsenic, which he used to poison rivals and enemies.

While the party were camping and waiting for a council with the "Mahar" (Omaha) Indians, an odd form of fishing was practiced. Some of the men made a drag of willows and bark and swept the creek hard by, catching hundreds of pike, bass, fish resembling salmon trout, red horse, buffalo fish, rockfish, perch, and catfish.

The Ottoe Indians of the first council then reappeared with others. They were asked to explain their trouble with the Omahas, which proved to be due to their desire to avenge the death of their brethren of the Missouris, who had been killed by the Omahas while attempting to steal horses. The only result of this conference was the distribution of more presents, since no Omahas had come, and a peace could not be arranged without them.

A little below Sioux City the first death occurred in the expedition. Sergeant Charles Floyd died of colic and was buried on a bluff about a mile below Floyd's River. Patrick Gass, who kept a journal of the expedition on his own account which was afterwards published, was elected sergeant in Floyd's place. Not far from this spot they learned that there was a quarry of red pipestone highly prized by the Indians for pipes.

The abundance of game which was then found in Nebraska, Iowa, and elsewhere along the route, is indicated by the record of August 23. "On the north side [this is properly the east side of the river] is an extensive and delightful prairie, which we called Buffalo prairie, from our having here killed our first buffalo. Two elk swam the river to-day and were fired at, but escaped; a deer was killed from the boat; one beaver was killed, and several prairie-wolves were seen."

CHAPTER XII

IN SOUTH DAKOTA

A haunted mountain. Among the Sioux. A curious fraternity. Some new animals. Trouble with the Tetons. The first meeting with the grizzly bear. Reaching the Arikara[1] Indians. The approach of cold weather.

By late August the explorers were entering the present South Dakota. There they examined a singularly symmetrical mound in the middle of the plains. The Indians believed this mound to be the abode of little spirits or devils not over eighteen inches in height, with large heads, and armed with bows and arrows which were always ready for use against any one who should approach. But Lewis and Clark "saw none of these wicked little spirits,

[1]"Aricaris, commonly called Rickarees, Rickrees, or Rees. The accepted spelling is now Arikara."—Coues's "Lewis and Clark," Vol. I, p. 143. In the journal this is spelled Rickara.

or any place for them except some small holes scattered over the top." This tradition is preserved in the modern name of Spirit Mound, which is in Clay County, South Dakota.

They were in the country of the formidable Sioux Indians, and the travelers set the prairie on fire as a notification of their coming. A few days later Sergeant Pryor and others were sent to the Sioux. On his return Pryor reported that the Sioux received them well and wished to carry them on a buffalo robe, an honor

TOTEM OF THE SIOUX

which they declined. They were also feasted on "a fat dog, already cooked, of which they partook heartily." This feast of dog meat was to be a frequent experience.

On August 30 Lewis and Clark received the Sioux chiefs and warriors in state, and gave them good advice regarding their relations with the United States. In addition to the usual presents the head chief received a richly laced artillery coat, and a cocked hat with a red feather. Then they all smoked the pipe of peace, and the young men shot at marks. At night the Indians held a dance, which was a new and striking spectacle for the white men.

The next day the Sioux chiefs made speeches in reply, which were peaceful, but their main

CALUMET, OR PIPE OF PEACE

point was that they wanted powder and ball, and presents for their squaws. More presents were given, and they promised to make peace with the Ottoes and Missouris.

In describing these Yankton Sioux the journal speaks of an association of young men among them who are bound never to retreat before any danger or give way to their enemies.

"In war they go forward without sheltering themselves behind trees. This determination not to be turned aside became heroic, or ridiculous, a short time since when the Yanktons were crossing the Missouri on the ice. A hole lay immediately in their course which might easily have been avoided by going around. This the leader of the band disdained to do, but went straight forward and was lost. The others would have followed his example but were forcibly prevented."

Above Yankton the explorers found great sand ridges so regular in their formation that they are described and mapped out in the journals as fortifications made by the hand of man. These were really only sand drifts, formed by the action of the river.

Another experience was the first glimpse of an antelope, which was called a goat. The Americans had never seen a prairie dog, and when they discovered a prairie-dog village they "poured five barrels of water into one of the holes without filling it, but we dislodged and caught the owner."

A noteworthy relic of a dead animal was found in the form of a "backbone of a fish forty-five feet long, in a perfect state of petrifaction." This was not a fish, but the remains of one of the extinct giant reptiles of the Cretaceous period.

The travelers saw buffalo, elk, "goats,"— or rather antelopes,—black-tailed deer, prairie wolves, coyotes, porcupines, rabbits, and barking squirrels, as they advanced. Captain Lewis tried to approach and shoot some antelopes, but in spite of his care they "fled with a speed equal to

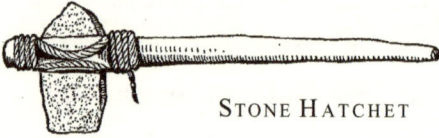

STONE HATCHET

that of the most distinguished race horse."

Although still within the present South Dakota the explorers by late September had reached the country of the Teton Sioux. While they were in Presho County a horse was stolen by the Sioux, and this annoyance was followed by a council meeting, which was very different from those held before. After the usual talk and present giving, the ungrateful

Sioux chief exclaimed that he had not received presents enough, and would stop the explorers. He "was proceeding to offer personal violence to Captain Clark, who immediately drew his sword and made a signal to the boat to prepare for action. The Indians who surrounded him drew their arrows from their quivers, and were bending their bows when the swivel [gun] was instantly pointed towards them and twelve of our most determined men jumped into the pirogue [small boat] and joined Captain Clark. This movement made an impression on them, for the grand chief ordered the young men away."

The courage and tact of the Americans resulted in a reconciliation. The next day Lewis and Clark were carried by the Sioux in a buffalo robe to the council house, where they smoked the pipe of peace; and a repast was served which consisted of dog and "pemitigon [pemmican],—a dish made of buffalo meat dried or jerked and then pounded and mixed raw with grease,—and a kind of ground potato dressed like the preparation of Indian corn called hominy, to which it is little inferior. Of all these luxuries which were placed before us in platters, with horn spoons, we took the pemitigon and the potato, which we found good; but we could as yet partake but sparingly of the dog."

Here they saw a scalp dance, and were fairly deafened by the noise of the drums. They noted every detail of Sioux life about them; saw the buffalo-skin lodges, the punishment of wrongdoers by officers appointed by the chief, noted the Indians themselves, with their heads shaven except for the scalp lock, their faces painted with grease and coal, and their robes of buffalo skin adorned with porcupine quills.

In spite of the Sioux professions of friendship they became troublesome again. They held the boat until the soldiers made ready to fire; then followed with others along the bank, alternately threatening and begging, until finally this rascally tribe was left behind and the expedition passed into the country of the Arikaras.

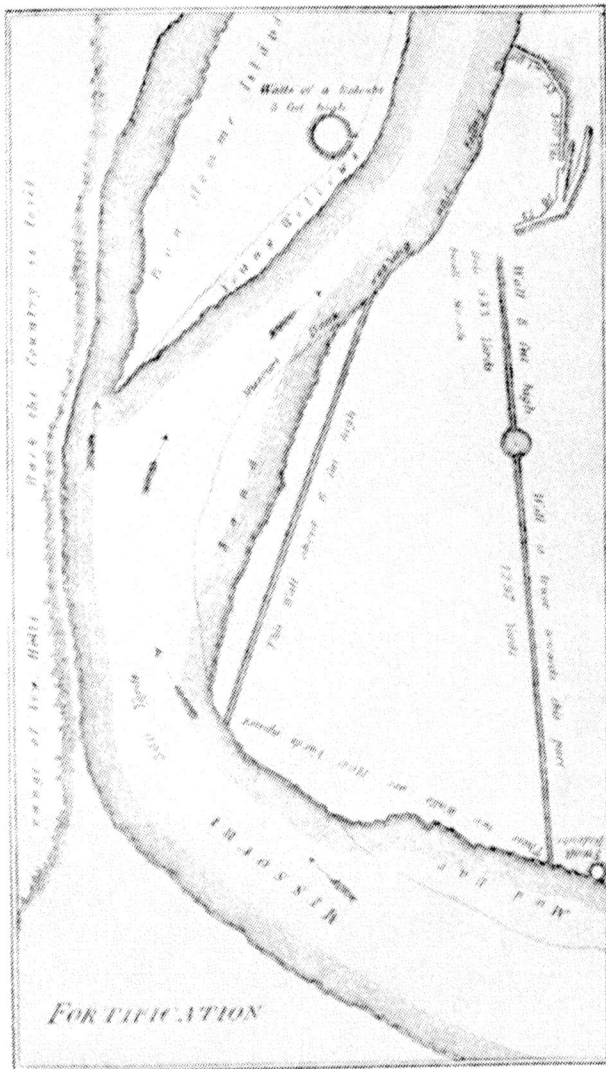

NATURE'S "FORTIFICATIONS"
(From the plan drawn by Lewis and Clark)

Here there were not only "goats" and "prairie cocks" but "white bear." This was the famous grizzly bear. The explorers also saw "a species of animal which resembled a small elk, with large, circular horns." This was the Rocky Mountain sheep, or bighorn. French fur traders were found as far in the wilderness as this, and they aided the travelers in calling a council, which differed from the others in one respect,—the Arikaras very sensibly refused whisky, saying that it would make them fools.

It was now October, and the weather was growing cold. The friendly Arikaras were left behind them, and on October 21 they reached a creek then called "Chisshetaw," and now Heart River, which joins the Missouri opposite the city of Bismarck, North Dakota, where the Northern Pacific Railroad now crosses the Missouri. The future site of Bismarck was then occupied by villages of the Mandan Indians. Since the cold weather would soon stop their progress it had been decided that they would winter among the Mandans.

CHAPTER XIII

AT THE MANDAN VILLAGES

The winter camp. Hunting the buffalo. The journey onward. Finding the Yellowstone River. Adventures with grizzly bears. Hunting in Montana.

On the north bank of the Missouri, in the present McLean County, North Dakota, about eight miles below the mouth of Big Knife

A MANDAN HUT

River, where the town of Stanton is now situated, the explorers built two rows of log huts, protected by a stockade, for their winter camp. The roofs were rudely thatched with grass and clay, and in spite of the bitter weather they "passed the winter comfortably."

Here they secured an Indian interpreter named Chaboneau. His wife, Sacajawea (Bird Woman), had been captured from the Snake Indians and sold to her husband. The journal speaks of her as "a good creature, of a mild and gentle disposition, greatly attached to the whites." She and her husband accompanied the travelers throughout the remainder of their journey, and her patience, courage, and helpfulness were unfailing.

The Sioux and other Indians were constantly engaged in warfare, and the Mandans suffered so much that Captain Clark once mustered twenty-four men and offered to lead the Mandans against the Sioux. The deep snow prevented, but the offer was gratefully received and remembered. The friendliest relations prevailed between these Indians and the explorers.

In December, Clark and others joined the Mandans in a great buffalo hunt. "The hunters, mounted on horseback and armed with

bows and arrows, encircle the herd and grad-
ually drive them into a plain. . . . They then
ride in and singling out a buffalo, a female
being preferred, go as close as possible and
wound her with arrows till they think they
have given the mortal stroke, when they
pursue another. If, which rarely happens,
the wounded buffalo attacks the hunter, he
evades his blow by the agility of his horse,
which is trained for the combat with great
dexterity."

In spite of weather so cold that the mercury
often went thirty-two degrees below zero,
the Indians kept up outdoor sports. Even the
white men enjoyed a merry Christmas. Later,
when their meat supply grew low, a hunting
expedition was sent out, which killed forty
deer, sixteen elk, and three buffalo. Although
the game was lean and the wolves stole much
of it, they gathered, in all, some three thousand pounds of meat.

Visits from white fur traders and the in-
roads of the Sioux were among the incidents
of a winter which must, after all, have passed

MANDAN INDIANS USING "BULL BOATS" MADE OF BUFFALO HIDE

slowly. In late February, however, it was possible to cut the boats free from the ice and to begin preparing them for the onward journey.

On April 7, 1805, the soldiers who had been sent as escort, with the boatmen and one

INTERIOR OF DESERTED MANDAN HUT

interpreter, started back. They carried reports for President Jefferson, with stuffed animals, and skeletons, horns, skins, and articles of Indian dress. All these reached the President safely in course of time, and the specimens were exhibited at his home in Monticello.

On the same day, April 7, the expedition, now consisting of thirty-two persons, embarked in two large boats, or pirogues, and six canoes, and started on their way into a region practically unknown to white men. The messages which the explorers sent back at this point were the last word received from them until they returned in September, 1806. But Captain Lewis wrote, "Entertaining as I do the most confident hope of succeeding in a voyage which had formed a darling project of mine for the last ten years, I could but esteem this moment of our departure as among the most happy of my life."

As they advanced they saw quantities of "brant" (snow geese), and they found an animal strange to them, the gopher. The squaw Sacajawea dug into some of the gopher holes and obtained wild artichokes collected by the gophers. The statement of Lewis and Clark that the wild geese which they saw built their nests in the tops of tall cottonwood trees was doubted at the time, but was nevertheless true. The travelers were now in the country of the sagebrush and alkali dust,—both unknown to them, and the latter very painful to their eyes.

They had heard of a large river as rising in the mountains and emptying into the Missouri, and on April 25 Captain Lewis and four men left the party and found the river, which was already known to French trappers, who called it *La Roche Jaune.* Captain Lewis named it the Yellowstone. It has kept the name, which is familiar also as the name of the National Park, in which the river rises. The wonders of the Yellowstone Park were discovered later by John Colter, then with the expedition.

They saw numbers of wild animals; and one day Captain Lewis, who was on shore with one hunter, encountered two of the formidable grizzly bears of which the Indians had given dreadful accounts. Both men "fired, and each wounded a bear; one of them made his escape; the other turned upon Captain Lewis and pursued him seventy or eighty yards, but being badly wounded could not run so fast as to prevent him from reloading his piece, which he again aimed at the bear, and a third shot from the hunter brought him to the ground."

A little later it was Captain Clark's turn. The huge bear which he met is called "brown," but the grizzly is called both "white" and "brown" in the journal. As the hunters fired, "the bear fled with a most tremendous roar, and such was his extraordinary tenacity of life that, although he had five balls passed through his lungs, and five other wounds, he swam more than half across the river to a sand bar and survived twenty minutes. He weighed between five and six hundred pounds at least, and measured eight feet seven inches and a half from the nose to the extremity of the hind feet."

At another time one of the men shot a grizzly through the lungs; but in spite of this wound the bear "pursued him furiously for over half a mile, then returned more than twice that distance and with his talons prepared himself a bed in the earth," where he was found and killed.

Another wounded grizzly pursued two hunters so closely that "they threw aside their guns and pouches, and jumped down a perpendicular bank of twenty feet into the river; the bear sprang after them and was within a few feet of the hindmost when one of the hunters on shore shot him in the head and finally killed him. They found that eight balls had passed through him in different directions."

When these exciting adventures happened they were journeying through Montana. They passed Porcupine River, named from the prevalence of those animals. This is now Poplar River, and there is an Indian agency at its mouth. They discovered Milk River, which keeps the name that they gave it on account of the whiteness of its water. They found a river bed without water, which they called "Big Dry," a name which is also preserved.

Again and again they speak of the quantities of buffalo and of elk. Now the few buffalo in the United States are guarded in the Yellowstone National Park and in zoölogical gardens and private preserves. Lewis and Clark found over a hundred skeletons of buffalo under a precipice over which they had been driven by the Indians.

There are still many elk in parts of the Rocky Mountains, but they are in danger of being destroyed like the buffalo. They are exposed not only to the ravages of hunters but also to the danger of starvation. In the winter of 1902–1903, when deep snow covered the grass, elk in Wyoming and elsewhere fairly stormed the haystacks of ranchers in their eagerness for food, and many died of starvation. The preservation of elk and other "big game" left in the West becomes yearly of greater importance.

CHAPTER XIV

ACROSS MONTANA

Discovery of the Musselshell. The first glimpse of the Rockies. A buffalo charges the camp. A narrow escape.
At the Great Falls of the Missouri. A difficult portage.
Reaching the Three Forks of the Missouri. In an unknown country.

This was a journey of incidents and accidents. At one time the explorers were startled
by the upsetting of the canoe containing their
papers, instruments, and medicines; but these
were fortunately saved. Again, they had a
narrow escape from being crushed by a falling tree. But they kept steadily on their
way, paddling, sailing when the wind per-
mitted, and sometimes towing the boats with
a line from shore.

On May 20 they reached the mouth of a
large river, the "Muscleshell" (Musselshell),
twenty-two hundred and seventy miles above

137

the Missouri's mouth. Thus another important river was discovered, although it was impossible to explore it. The information given by Indians, that it rose in the mountains near the source of the Yellowstone, was erroneous.

On May 26, 1805, when the party had reached the present Cow Creek, Montana, Captain Lewis, after ascending the highest summit of some hills, "first caught a distant view of the Rock mountains, the object of all our hopes and the reward of all our ambition." It was a thrilling moment for the explorers; but they were not the first, for the Verendryes had seen the Rocky Mountains many years before.

A few days later a frightened buffalo broke into the camp at night. He galloped close to the heads of the men as they lay asleep by the camp fires, and nearly broke into the officers' lodge. He was turned by the barking of a dog and, wheeling, vanished in the darkness before the men realized what had happened.

Early in June, when the explorers were near the site of the present town of Ophir,

Montana, they came to a large stream which they called Maria's River. It was so large that they were in doubt as to whether this river from the southwest or the main stream from the north was the real Missouri. "On our right decision," says the journal, "much of the fate of the expedition depends: since if, after ascending to the Rocky Mountains or beyond them, we should find that the river we were following did not come near the Columbia and be obliged to return, we should not only lose the traveling season, but probably dishearten the men."

To determine this point Captain Lewis started to explore the north fork, and Captain Clark the south. In three days Lewis was persuaded that his fork extended too far north for an approach to the Columbia, and he turned back.

Here there was a narrow escape from a serious accident. While passing along a bluff his foot slipped, and he barely saved himself with his spontoon (pike) from falling ninety feet, over a precipice into the river. Suddenly he heard one of his men cry, "Captain, what shall I do?" and turning saw the man lying on the edge of the precipice, his right arm and leg over the brink. Lewis was self-possessed. He told the man to take out his knife with his right hand and dig a hole in which he could place his right foot. Thus by degrees the poor fellow worked his way to safety.

Lewis and Clark of course were right in deciding that the northerly stream—Marias River—was a tributary, and that the southwestern stream was the Missouri. But many of the party thought differently, including Crusatte, an experienced *voyageur*. So they decided to explore farther. Digging holes in the ground, they concealed many of their goods in *caches* (the French name for these places for hiding stores from Indians and wild animals). Lewis ascended the south branch, the real Missouri, and on June 13 all doubts were set at rest by his discovery of the Great Falls of the Missouri, which the Indians had described. Of this wonderful cataract he gives a vivid picture. But his enjoyment of the beautiful sight and his further investigations were suddenly interrupted. A large grizzly bear charged upon him while his gun was unloaded, and chased him into the river. There the bear fortunately left him standing in water waist deep, with pike presented. Whatever Captain Lewis's dreams may have been that night his waking must have been equally disturbing, for when he opened his eyes he saw a large rattlesnake coiled about the trunk of the tree under which he had been sleeping.

It was necessary to make a portage to transport their boats and baggage around the succession of cataracts and rapids. The south side of the river was selected for a portage path eighteen miles in length. The clearing of this long path was one of the many examples of the hard work done by the explorers. In addition, Captain Clark made careful surveys and maps of the falls, cascades, and rapids. A few years ago, when a manufacturing company planned a dam at one of the falls, their engineers found Captain Clark's surveys entirely accurate. The total fall of the river is 412.5 feet, and the Great Falls alone plunges down 75.5 feet.

It was not until June 27 that the portage path was finished, after much hard work, and much annoyance from the prickly pear, which pierced their moccasins. They had other adventures with bears, which, with elk, were plentiful then. At this haunt of wild animals there is to-day Great Falls,—a town of over ten thousand people.

After hiding or *caching* such articles as could be left behind, the weary task of carrying their supplies over the long portage was begun. Suddenly there was a cloud-burst and a flow of water, from which Sacajawea, the faithful Snake Indian woman who accompanied her husband the guide from the Mandan villages, was barely saved by Clark, who was himself in great danger. But the work was done, in spite of a hailstorm and the annoyances of bears, and swarms of peculiarly active mosquitoes.

At the head of the falls a disappointment awaited them. An iron frame for a boat had been brought all the way from Harpers Ferry, Virginia. Over this frame they fastened the dressed skins of buffaloes and elks, covering the seams with beeswax mixed with powdered charcoal. But on launching the boat they found that this did not protect the seams, and the boat leaked so badly that they were forced to abandon it. It was therefore necessary to make canoes. Trees were scarce, and Clark traveled many miles before he found two cottonwoods which seemed suitable. But on cutting them down they were found to be partly hollow and damaged in falling. With the perseverance and pluck which showed in everything that these men did, they wrought out the best canoes they could, although their ax handles, which were made on the spot, were constantly breaking as they worked.

On July 15 they again set out upon their journey with eight heavily laden canoes. They encountered projecting cliffs, which sometimes made them pass and repass from one side of the river to the other. They noted fields of sunflowers, the seeds of which the Indians used to make bread. They found purple, yellow, and black currants, and many other berries, and on the cliffs they saw bighorns or Rocky Mountain sheep. Advancing through a frowning cañon which they called the "Gates of the Rocky Mountains," they continued southward with the Big Belt Mountains on the east and the main range of the Rockies on the west.

They were anxious to find some Shoshone or Snake Indians in order to obtain guides and horses; but the first Indians that they came near were frightened away by the guns of the hunters, and set the grass on fire as a sign of danger for their companions.

On July 25 Captain Clark, who was ahead, reached the Three Forks of the Missouri. The one flowing northeast, which is the main Missouri, was named the Jefferson. The name of Madison, the Secretary of State, was given to the middle branch, and the third was named for Albert Gallatin, Secretary of the Treasury. These names have been preserved. At this point the explorers were to the eastward of the present cities of Helena and Butte. Not

far away, over the divide between southern
Montana and Idaho, were the sources of some
streams flowing to the Pacific. But this they
had yet to learn. They were in a country
untrodden by white men, a country of which
they could obtain only vague ideas from the
Indians, and yet much depended upon getting
into communication with them. The explorers
wished to find a pass through the mountains,
and although Sacajawea was now in her own
land, her knowledge of what lay beyond was
very slight, and the real guaranty of success
lay in the stout hearts, cheerful courage, and
dauntless perseverance of the explorers themselves.

CHAPTER XV

THROUGH THE ROCKIES TO THE PACIFIC

Ascending the Jefferson. Reaching the Great Divide. Some
  friendly Indians. Sacajawea meets old acquaintances.
  Hardships and disappointments. Struggling across the
  mountains. Among the Nez Percés. On toward the sea.
  Passing the cataracts of the Columbia. The first glimpse
  of the sea.

It was on the 30th of July that they began
the laborious ascent of the Jefferson, or true
Missouri. Captain Lewis went ahead to find
some Indians and gain information as to the
way across the mountains. The others followed, struggling with rapids and shoals, often
wading through the water over slippery stones
and dragging the boats, and often puzzled as
to the right course by the bewildering forks
of the stream. On August 11 Lewis saw a
Shoshone on horseback, whom he tried vainly
to attract by holding up a looking-glass and

beads and making friendly signs. Lewis was now traveling near the base of the Bitter Root Mountains, hoping to find an Indian trail leading to a pass. As he kept on, the Jefferson grew smaller and smaller, until it dwindled to a brook, and one of the men, with a foot on each side, "thanked God that he had lived to bestride the Missouri."

They had then found and were following an Indian trail, and at last they came to a gap in the mountains where they drank from the actual source of the great Missouri River, which they had ascended from its mouth.

The Indian trail brought them to the top of a ridge commanding snow-topped mountains to the westward. "The ridge on which they stood formed the dividing line between the waters of the Atlantic and Pacific oceans. The descent was much steeper than on the eastern side, and at the distance of three-quarters of a mile they reached a bold creek of cold, clear water running west, and stopped to taste for the first time the waters of the Columbia."

These were the first white men to cross the "Continental Divide" in our Northwest. In 1792–1793 Alexander Mackenzie had crossed British America to the Pacific.

Lewis and his men kept on to the westward and finally made friends with some Indians.

MAP OF LEWIS AND CLARK PASS

They smoked the pipe of peace and partook of a salmon,—another proof that they were on the Pacific side of the mountains. The chief promised horses but afterward became suspicious of some treachery, and, between the chief's changes of mind and scanty food, Lewis's stay was made most uncomfortable. But at last he and the Indians, with horses, started back to meet Captain Clark, who all this time had been laboriously ascending the Jefferson with the boats.

On August 17, after retracing his course across the divide, Captain Lewis and his party found Captain Clark. As they approached each other the faithful Sacajawea, who was with Clark, began to dance with joy, pointing to the Indians and sucking her fingers to show that they were of her tribe. Presently an Indian woman came to her, and they embraced each other with the most tender affection. "They had been companions in childhood; in the war with the Minnetarees they had both been taken prisoners in the same battle; they had shared and softened the rigors of their captivity till one of them had escaped from their enemies with scarce a hope of ever seeing her friend rescued from their hands."

It was arranged that Clark, with eleven men and with tools, should cross the divide to the village of the Shoshonees. He was then to lead his men down the Columbia and, when he found navigable water, to begin to build canoes.

Lewis was to remain and bring the baggage to the Shoshone village. At the council held here the Indians promised to bring more horses, and showed great astonishment at the arms and dress of the men, the "strange looks" of the negro, and the air gun.

On August 20 Clark reached the Shoshone village, which since Lewis's visit had been moved two miles up the little river on which it was situated. Here he heard most discouraging accounts of the wild country before him and the difficulty of reaching navigable water by which they could descend to the sea. These stories proved too true. Clark passed the junction of the Salmon and Lemhi rivers, where Salmon City, Idaho, is now situated, and he gave the name of Lewis River to the stream below the junction.

The traveling over rocky mountain paths was most trying, and instead of the abundance of game which they had seen in Montana and Dakota there was an absence of deer and other animals. They were obliged to depend largely on such salmon as they could catch, or buy

from the Indians. Since the Indians themselves were scant of food, and the white men
had no proper fishing tackle, it is not strange
that Clark's followers began to fear starvation. They explored the Salmon River for
fifty-two miles, but saw that progress that way
was impossible, and, unsuccessful for once,
they returned to join Lewis.

Meantime Lewis had had his own troubles.
After promising horses and aid, the Indians
threatened to leave him for a buffalo hunt on
the eastern side of the mountains, and it was
only by much tact and patience that he kept
them with him.

On August 30 Clark returned from his unsuccessful search for a water way. A part
of the baggage was hidden and the rest was
packed on horses. Then the explorers went
on slowly through the Bitter Root Mountains.
The Indian guide lost his way completely.
"The thickets through which we were obliged
to cut our way required great labor; the road
itself was over the steep and rocky sides of
the hills, where the horses could not move

without danger of slipping down, while their feet were bruised by the rocks and stumps." They saw no game, and were obliged to resort to horseflesh for food. The nights were cold, and as they reached greater heights the trail was sometimes covered with snow. A few cans of soup and twenty pounds of bear's oil were all the food that they had left. No wonder that the men grew weak and ill.

But on September 20, half-starved and sick, after nearly three weeks of hardships in the Bitter Root Mountains, they emerged upon a plain where they found Indians and food. At last the barrier of the mountains had been broken through.

These Indians were the Nez Percés. Among the articles of food which they offered were various roots, including the *quamash,* which was ground and made into a cake called *pasheco.* This root is still eaten by the Nez Percés, and from quamash comes the name of Camas Prairie. It seemed a relief to have a comparative abundance of food. But this consisted principally of fish and roots, and this strange diet, of which they naturally ate heartily after their privations, caused serious illness throughout the party. "Captain Lewis could hardly sit on his horse, while others were obliged to be put on horseback, and some, from extreme weakness and pain, were forced to lie down alongside of the road for some time."

While resting at the Nez Percé village near the present Pierce City, Idaho, they learned all that they could of the country beyond. The Indian chief Twisted-hair drew a rude map of the rivers, showing the forks of the Kooskooskee, now the Clearwater, the junction with the Snake River, and the entrance of another large river, which was the Columbia.

Late in September, after obtaining provisions from the Indians, they moved on to a camp on the Kooskooskee River. In spite of continued illness they built five canoes. They concealed some of their goods, left their horses with the Indians, and, undaunted by their sufferings, started down the river in their canoes on October 8. One canoe was sunk by striking a rock, and a halt was called to dry the luggage and make repairs. Fish and even dogs were bought from the Indians for food.

Always alert for information, the explorers noted all the peculiarities of their hosts. There were the baths, or sweat houses, which were hollow squares in the river banks, where the bather steamed himself by pouring water on heated stones. Some of the Indians cooked salmon by putting hot stones into a bucket of water until it would boil the fish. Many of them were frightened by the coming of the white men with their guns. At one place Captain Clark, unperceived by them, shot a white crane, and seeing it fall they believed it to be the white men descending from the clouds. When Clark used his burning glass to light his pipe they were more than ever sure that their visitors were not mortal. But they were finally reassured by presents and the kindness and tact which the travelers showed in all their dealings with the savages. There were "almost inconceivable multitudes of salmon" in the rivers. Many at that season were floating down stream, and the Indians were collecting, splitting, and drying them on scaffolds.

One of the first camps was at the junction of the Kooskooskee and Snake, where the city of Lewiston, Idaho, now stands,—named for Captain Lewis. Then, entering the present state of Washington, they descended the Snake, where the wind and the rapids caused various accidents. On October 16 they reached the mighty Columbia, which had been called by the Indians the "Oregon," or "River of the West." This was to be their pathway to the sea.

They were now among the Sokulk Indians, from whom they purchased more dogs, since the salmon were poor and they had accustomed themselves to dog flesh. They noted the deerskin robes of the red men, and their method of gigging (spearing) salmon and drying them; the prevalence of sore eyes among the Indians, ascribed to the glare from the water; and their bad teeth, which they traced to a diet of gritty roots.

On October 23, two days after their first glimpse of Mt. Hood, they reached the first

falls of the Columbia, which they passed successfully by portages and by letting the canoes
down the rapids with lines. At the next fall
they managed, after partially unloading the
canoes, to run them down through a narrow
passage, past a high, black rock, much to the
astonishment of the Indians.

Here they were surprised to find that the
savages (Echeloots, related to the Upper Chinooks) were living in wooden houses, which
consisted in large part of an underground
room, lined with wood and covered above
ground with a roof composed of ridgepole,
rafters, and a white cedar covering. Here, as
before, the explorers acted the part of peacemakers, and urged the Indians to cease their
warfare with neighboring tribes. Lewis and
Clark had before this seen flat-headed women
and children in certain tribes, but here the
men also had been subjected to this cruel
practice. The result was often accomplished
by binding a board tightly on an infant's
forehead, and thus flattening it backward and
upward.

On October 28 they were visited by an Indian "who wore his hair in a *que* [cue] and had on a round hat and a sailor's jacket which he said he had obtained from the people below the great rapids, who bought them from the whites." This was a cheering indication of their approach to the mouth of the Columbia, where the fur trade attracted American and English ships. Later they found an English musket and cutlass and some brass teakettles in an Indian hut, and one of the chiefs had cloths and a sword procured from some English vessel.

Thus they went on through the present Skamania County, Washington, hunting now and then with some slight success, observing the country, buying roots and dogs, and making notes of the habits of the natives and of their burial places, until they came to the "great shoot" or last rapids of the Columbia, which they passed without serious accident.

From Indians below the rapids they heard the encouraging news that three ships had lately been seen at the mouth of the river.

As they journeyed toward the sea, the entrance of the Multnomah, now the Willamette River, was concealed from them by the islands at its mouth. A few miles farther up, the prosperous city of Portland, Oregon, now stands. While they were being piloted down the river by the Indian who had come to them in a sailor's jacket, they caught sight of Mt. St. Helens.

Fog and rain, thievish Indians, and the noises of wild fowl at night were among their smaller troubles, but all were forgotten when, on November 7, the fog suddenly cleared away and "we enjoyed the delightful prospect of the ocean,—that ocean, the object of all our labors, the reward of all our anxieties. This cheering view exhilarated the spirits of all the party, who were still more delighted on hearing the distant roar of the breakers."

Remembering what they had undergone, one can understand their joy at success in their perilous task. They had crossed the continent.

CHAPTER XVI

ON THE PACIFIC SLOPE

The winter camp. Peculiarities of the Clatsop Indians. A
scarcity of supplies. Turning homeward. Surmounting
the cascades. Journeying by land. Troublesome Indians.
Living on dog flesh. A search for their horses. Indian
cooking. Suffering of the explorers.

The sea gave them an inhospitable welcome.
As they neared a camping place which they
selected on Gray's Bay, in Wahkiakum County,
Washington, the waves were so high that some
of the men became seasick. Next day they
were beaten back to camp by the rough
water, which their canoes, mere dugouts, could
not withstand. They were flooded by inces-
sant rain and harassed by heavy winds, thievish Indians, and the fleas which were the
Indians' constant companions.

At their next camp, on Baker's Bay, they
suffered even more from the merciless rain.

159

They found game, and explored to some extent the mouth of the Columbia. They hoped to encounter a trading ship from which they could replenish their stores, but none appeared. It was necessary to find a place for a winter camp and Lewis finally discovered one, on the south side of the Columbia, not far from their present camp. Before leaving the latter this inscription was carved on the trunk of a lofty pine:

> "Wm. Clark December 3 D 1805
> By Land from the U. States
> in 1804 & 5."

Some three miles up the Netul River, which empties into a bay named Meriwether's (for Captain Meriwether Lewis), they made their camp on a bluff in a grove of lofty pines. There they built seven log cabins, roofed with rude shingles, or more properly slabs, called "shakes," which were split from pine logs. Their meat house was replenished by hunting elk and deer. In the course of the winter they killed one hundred and thirty-one of the former and twenty of the latter.

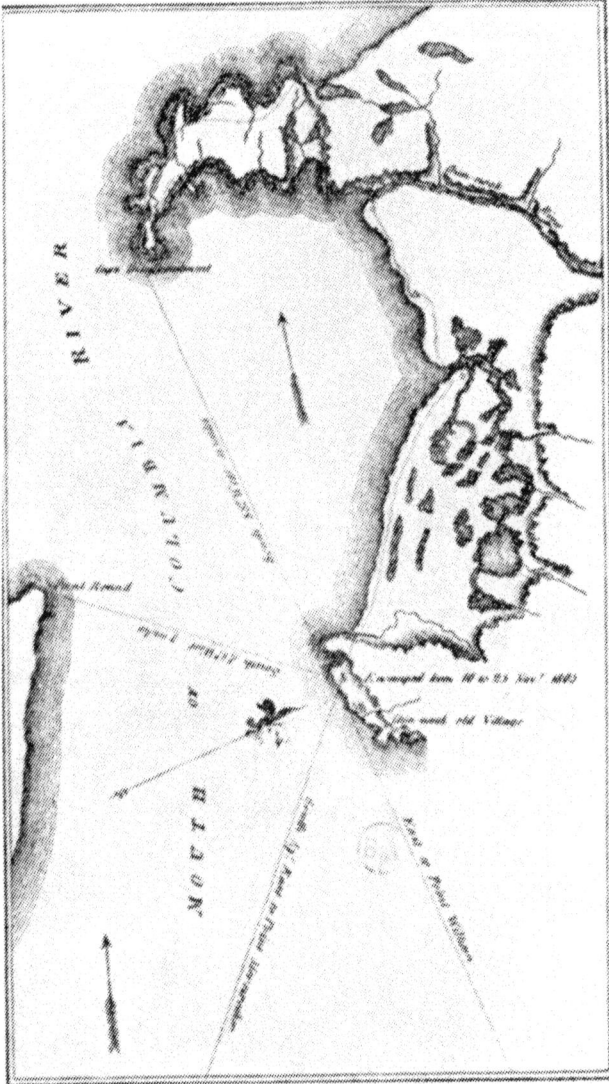

MOUTH OF THE COLUMBIA RIVER
(From the plan drawn by Lewis and Clark)

They saw much of the Clatsop Indians, who lived in houses of split pine boards half above and half below the ground. The explorers noted that these Indians were cleanly and frequently washed their faces and hands, something which they had rarely seen among other tribes. In their most common game "one of the party had a piece of bone about the size of a large bean, and having agreed with any individual as to the value of the stake, he would pass the bone from one hand to the other with great dexterity, singing at the same time to divert the attention of his adversary; then holding it in his closed hands, his antagonist was challenged to guess in which of them the bone was." This seems to have been a variety of the game, "Button, Button, who has the Button?"

These Clatsops are described as wearing hats "made of cedar-bark and bear-grass, interwoven together in the form of a European hat, with a small brim of about two inches, and a high crown widening upward. They are light, ornamented with various colors, and being nearly waterproof, are much more durable than either chip or straw hats. . . . But the most curious workmanship is that of the basket. It is formed of cedar-bark and bear-grass, so closely interwoven that it is water-tight, without the aid of either gum or resin."

These Indians were much more attractive than the dwarfish and ugly Chinooks, whom they also observed, but with great caution on account of their thievish habits.

The winter was not eventful. They hunted, studied the Indians, and made salt by evaporating sea water. There was little snow, but the rain was persistent.

In March they prepared for their long journey homeward. On examining their stores they found a sufficient supply of powder. This was in leaden canisters, which, when they had been emptied, were melted to make bullets. Their goods, however, were nearly exhausted. "All the small merchandise we possess might be tied up in a couple of handkerchiefs. The rest of our stock in trade consists of six blue robes, one scarlet robe, five robes which we made of our United States flag, a few old clothes trimmed with ribbons, and one artillerist's coat and hat, which probably Captain Clark will never wear again. We have to depend entirely upon this meagre outfit for the purchase of such horses and provisions as it will be in our power to obtain—a scant dependence indeed, for such a journey as is before us."

Before they started they made several copies of a list of the party, a map of their route, and a memorandum regarding their travels. These they left with the Clatsops, who were to give them to any white man. One list was given the next summer to Captain Hill of the brig *Lydia,* who came to the coast to trade. He took it to China and then sent it to the United States, where it arrived safely.

At this point in the journal there is a long and careful account of all the plants, animals, birds, and fish which they had seen, showing how thoroughly they had studied the natural history of the country during the winter.

On March 23, 1806, the canoes were loaded and they began the journey eastward. The hunters of the party searched the shores diligently for game with some success. They obtained "wappatoo" (arrowhead roots) from the various Indians whom they met, some of whom, the Skilloots, were old acquaintances, and later, dogs were again necessary to help out their fare. On the return, Captain Clark discovered the Multnomah, now the Willamette River, which as we have seen they failed to notice on the descent. They describe Mt. Hood and Mt. Regnier (Rainier), St. Helens, and Mt. Jefferson, and they note the beautiful cascades along the rocky walls of the Columbia, among them the superb Multnomah Falls.

On April 9 they reached Beacon Rock on the north side of the river, which marks the head of tide water and the foot of the cascades of the Columbia. They had only one towrope, and it was therefore a long and tiresome task to drag the canoes one by one along the shore to the portage. Here they were obliged to unload the canoes and carry

Copyright, 1901, by Detroit Photographic
Company

MULTNOMAH FALLS

their effects around. The Indians, Wahclel-
lahs, crowded about them and threatened violence. Some of them threw stones. Two
attempted to take a dog from Shields, one of
the men. "He had no weapon but a long
knife, with which he immediately attacked
both, hoping to put them to death before they
had time to draw their arrows; but as soon as
they saw his design they fled into the woods."

After much labor the company passed the
cascades, and presently surmounted the "Long
Narrows." These are now known as the
Dalles of the Columbia, from a French word
meaning flat stones. At the head is now
Celilo City, and at the foot Dalles City, both
in Oregon.

By April 16 the party reached the plains
stretching away to the foot of the Rockies,
and they found that the air was drier and
more pure, and that they had emerged from
the region of constant rains.

After various efforts a few horses were procured and some of the canoes were broken
up, and from the 24th of April they traveled

wholly by land. Their stock of goods was so
low that it was hard to trade for horses, and
on the 28th we find Captain Clark obliged to
give his sword for a white horse in addition
to some powder and ball.

The Skilloot Indians and others proved
thievish and disobliging. One of them was
kicked out of camp for stealing, but in spite
of these troubles bloodshed was avoided by tact
and patience. An agreeable contrast was afforded by the "Walla wollahs" (Walla Wallas),
three of whom travelled a whole day to return
a steel trap which the explorers had left behind. It is pleasant also to know that Lewis
and Clark were enabled by their knowledge
of medicine and surgery to help these Indians.
They set a broken arm and put it into splints,
and gave medicines to the sick. They enter-
tained other Indians with their violins, which
had been carefully preserved throughout their
vicissitudes.

They were now crossing the plains where
fuel and game were scarce. They passed
along the Walla Walla River in Washington

on their way toward the Kooskooskee River and their friends the Chopunnish Indians. Early in May they met an old acquaintance, Weahkoonut, who had guided them down the Snake in the previous autumn. The explorers had been living on scanty rations and were half famished, and they found that the Indians themselves were little better off. Dog flesh was their chief reliance until the hunters succeeded in killing some deer.

It will be remembered that they had left their horses with these Indians in the autumn and had hidden their saddles and some of their goods. But there had been quarrels among the Indians, the hiding place had been exposed, some of the saddles were gone, and it was only after much trouble that the horses were recovered.

On May 10 there was a heavy snowstorm, and as the mountains were covered the explorers made a camp on the river to await the melting of the snow. They were now on the Kooskooskee, in the Nez Percé County, Idaho, to the eastward of the city of Lewiston.

Here they held a grand council with the Indians, explaining the sovereignty and beneficent intentions of the United States. It would be hard to say exactly what ideas reached the Indians. The explorers spoke in English to one of their men. He translated the message into French for Chaboneau. He interpreted it to his wife in the Minnetaree language. She put it into Shoshone, and a young Shoshone prisoner among the Indians explained it to the Chopunnish in their own dialect. Whatever they might have gathered from the talk, the Indians had no difficulty in understanding the presents which were made them.

The hunters encountered grizzly bears again, and some meat was given to the Indians, which they cooked in an odd way. "They immediately prepared a large fire of dried wood, on which was thrown a number of smooth stones from the river. As soon as the fire burned down and the stones were heated, they were laid next to each other in a level position and covered with a quantity of pine branches, on which were placed flitches of the meat, and then boughs and flesh alternately for several courses, leaving a thick layer of pine on the top. On this heap they then poured a small quantity of water and covered the whole with earth to the depth of four inches. After remaining in this state for about three hours, the meat was taken off, and was really more tender than that which we had boiled or roasted, though the strong flavor of the pine rendered it disagreeable to our palates."

Their stay in this country was made uncomfortable by a recurrence of the rains. They often slept in pools of rain water. About the middle of May they found that the stores of each man were reduced to one awl, a knitting needle, half an ounce of vermillion, two needles, a few skeins of thread, and a yard of ribbon. This represented their means of trading with the Indians. To increase their store they cut from their ragged uniforms the brass buttons which attracted the Indians, and bought fish, bread, and roots. They also exchanged some of their eyewater and ointment, and tin boxes in which they had kept phosphorus.

The medical practice of the explorers continued. They treated the Chopunnish (Nez Percés) for sore eyes and for rheumatism. There was much sickness among their own party. However much they suffered themselves, they gave the tenderest care to one pathetic little figure,—a strange comrade for such a journey,—the baby of Sacajawea.

It was not a cheerful time that they passed at this camp. They gathered all the food possible, nursed their sick, cared for their horses, and waited as patiently as possible for the deep snow to melt, so that they might cross the mountains.

Once, on June 10, they started, but snow fifteen feet deep forced them to return, after several accidents. It was essential that they should descend the Missouri before winter closed navigation. Salt had given out, they were unable to catch fish, and there was no game until they returned to Quamash (Camas) Flats, where some deer and bears were killed. The explorers recorded these facts in their journal without complaints or despondency.

CHAPTER XVII

ACROSS THE MOUNTAINS

A rough mountain road. Dividing the party. An adventure
with a grizzly. Fighting with Indians. An accident to
Captain Lewis. His indomitable courage. Passing the
Great Falls of the Missouri. Lewis overtakes Captain
Clark.

On June 24, after securing some Indian
guides, they set out on a second attempt to
pass the mountains. This time, in spite of
snow, dangerous precipices, and steep ascents,
they succeeded in crossing the Bitter Root
range. They traveled one hundred and fifty-
six miles in this rough journey from Idaho
into Montana. On June 30 they reached
their old camp on Clark's River, Montana.

They decided that Lewis and nine men
should hasten on to the falls of the Missouri
and prepare for the portage of canoes and
baggage. Clark was to go to the head of the

Jefferson River, which Sergeant Ordway and nine men were to descend, while Clark and ten men were to descend the Yellowstone. This was in order to gain as much knowledge as possible of the country.

Lewis's journey to the falls was uneventful. There were plenty of elk and other game, and also, unfortunately, of mosquitoes. On opening their cache at the falls they found the bearskins and specimens of plants spoiled by water. Some of the horses disappeared, and Drewyer, the mightiest hunter of the party, went on a long and fruitless quest for them. Another man, M'Neal, "approached a thicket in which there was a white [grizzly] bear which he did not discover until he was within ten feet of him; his horse started, and wheeling suddenly round, threw M'Neal almost immediately under the bear. He started up instantly, and finding the bear raising himself on his hind feet to attack him, struck him on the head with the butt of his musket. The blow was so violent that it broke the breech of the musket and knocked the bear to the ground, and before he recovered, M'Neal, seeing a willow tree close by, sprang up it and there stayed, while the bear closely guarded the foot of the tree until late in the afternoon. He then went off and M'Neal, being released, came down."

After preparing the carriages for the boats, Lewis started northward to explore Marias River. They were in a buffalo country, and there were signs of Indians. This was the land of the troublesome Blackfoot and Minnetaree Indians, and the signs were disturbing. Lewis followed up the north fork of Marias River, known as the Cut-bank River, in the northwest corner of Montana. He was anxious to find whether its source was in British America or the United States. But cloudy weather prevented them from taking observations, and the chronometer stopped for a time and they found themselves unable to determine the longitude. Without exact observations they could not fix the boundary line. Finally they turned back, after naming the place Camp Disappointment.

On the same day, July 26, they encountered a band of eight Minnetarees armed with two guns and bows and arrows. At first the meeting was peaceful, but the white men knew that these Indians were treacherous and great horse thieves. They camped together, but Lewis himself kept on watch until a late hour and then woke one of his men. It was fortunate that they were vigilant. Toward morning the Indians quietly rose and seized the rifles. "As soon as Fields [the sentinel, who had carelessly laid aside his rifle] turned round, he saw the Indian running off with the rifles, and instantly calling his brother they pursued him for fifty or sixty yards, and just as they overtook him, in the scuffle for the rifles, R. Fields stabbed him through the heart with his knife; the Indian ran about fifteen steps and fell dead."

Meantime there was another struggle at the camp. An Indian had seized Drewyer's rifle, but on the instant Drewyer leaped up and wrested it from him. Awakened by the noise Captain Lewis reached for his rifle only to

Merewether Lewis

see an Indian running off with it. Drawing his pistol he rushed after the Indian, who finally threw the gun down. They had saved their rifles, but their horses were now in danger. Lewis ordered the men to pursue the main party, who were driving off most of the horses. He himself, bareheaded, ran after two Indians who were escaping with another horse. He shouted breathlessly that unless they returned it he would shoot, and shoot he did, wounding one of the Indians, who fired at him. "The shot had nearly been fatal, for Captain Lewis felt the wind of the ball very distinctly."

The result of this little battle was wholly favorable to the explorers. They lost one horse, but captured four Indian horses and some shields, bows, quivers, and one gun which the Indians left in the camp. The Indian killed by Fields was the one to whom they had presented a medal the day before, and this they left around his neck, "that they might be informed who we were." The patience and adroitness of the explorers had kept them almost wholly free from serious trouble with the Indians. In this case they were forced to act in self-defense.

Very naturally they lost no time in starting on, fearing immediate pursuit by a larger band, but they made the journey back to the falls of the Missouri in safety.

Lewis and his reunited party, who had been joined by Sergeant Ordway and his men, passed around the falls and hastened down the river. At the mouth of the Yellowstone they found a note from Captain Clark, who was waiting a few miles below. But before they overtook him their leader, Captain Lewis, narrowly escaped death. Landing with the canoeman, Cruzatte, to hunt some elk, they took different routes. "Just as Captain Lewis was taking aim at an elk, a ball struck him in the left thigh, about an inch below the joint of the hip, and, missing the bone, went through the left thigh, and grazed the right to the depth of the ball. It instantly occurred to him that Cruzatte must have shot him by mistake for an elk, as he was dressed in brown leather, and Cruzatte had not a very good eyesight."

He called to Cruzatte, but received no answer. Fearing an Indian ambush he pluckily made his way to the boat, shouting to Cruzatte to retreat. He reached the boat, and, wounded as he was, bravely led the men back to relieve Cruzatte. After a hundred steps his wound made it impossible for him to go on. Without thought of a guard for himself, he sent the men on, and "limping back to the boat, he prepared himself with his rifle, a pistol, and the air-gun, to sell his life dearly in case the men should be overcome."

After all, it was a false alarm as regarded the Indians. It was Cruzatte himself who had shot Captain Lewis. He had seen the brown suit and had mistaken him for an elk.

The suffering of Captain Lewis was none the less real as he lay in the bottom of the pirogue while they went on to overtake Captain Clark. On August 12 they met two fur traders from Illinois, and on the same day they joined Captain Clark, near the mouth of Little Knife Creek, and the whole party were reunited.

CHAPTER XVIII

CAPTAIN CLARK'S ADVENTURES

Crossing to the Yellowstone. The last glimpse of the Rockies. Buffalo and bears. Reaching the Missouri. Attacked by mosquitoes. Pryor loses the horses. Bitten by a wolf. The whole party reunited.

We must go back for more than a month to begin the story of Clark's exploration of the Yellowstone River. He had parted from the others on July 3 at Traveler's Rest Creek in the Bitter Root Mountains in western Montana. With fifteen men and Sacajawea, her child, and fifty horses, they traveled along Clark's River. On July 4, having made sixteen miles, "we halted at an early hour for the purpose of doing honor to the birthday of our country's independence. The festival was not very splendid, for it consisted of a mush made of cows [cowish] roots and a saddle of venison, nor had we anything to tempt us to prolong it."

178

In passing from the present Missoula County, Montana, into Beaver County they crossed a hill which divides the flow of water to the Atlantic from that to the Pacific. They discovered some of the hot sulphur springs which have since become so familiar. At the forks of the Jefferson they opened the cache made in August, 1805, and found the hidden goods and canoes generally in excellent condition. In their descent of the Jefferson they saw "innumerable quantities of beaver and otter, [and] the bushes of the low grounds are a favorite resort for deer, while on the higher parts of the valley are seen scattered groups of antelopes, and still further, on the steep sides of the mountains, we observed many of the big horn which take refuge there from the wolves and bear." This was to the westward of the present Bannock City.

When they reached the mouth of Madison River, Clark sent Sergeant Ordway and nine men on down the Missouri to overtake Lewis and the others. Clark himself, with ten men and Sacajawea, her baby, and fifty horses, set out from the forks of the Missouri to reach the Yellowstone River. The travelers of to-day who pass through Bozeman Pass from Gallatin City to Livingston by the railroad are following Captain Clark's route for much of the way.

Sacajawea, always helpful, found edible roots, and assisted the travelers by her recollections of the country. On July 15 they passed the ridge dividing the waters of the Missouri and the Yellowstone. Some of the horses were stolen by Indians in the night. One of the hunters "fell on a small piece of timber, which ran nearly two inches into the muscular part of his thigh. The wound was very painful, and were it not for their great anxiety to reach the United States this season, the party would have remained till he was cured." But it was necessary to place him in a rude litter and to press on. They reached a tributary of the Yellowstone, where they made two dugouts which were lashed together. Sergeant Pryor and two others were sent on with the horses, and the sergeant's experience was most unfortunate. "As soon as they discovered a herd of buffalo the loose horses, having been trained by the Indians to hunt, immediately set off in pursuit of them, and surrounded the buffalo herd with almost as much skill as their riders could have done. At last he was obliged to send one horseman forward and drive all the buffalo from the route." But the whole party aided in getting most of the horses across the river, and Pryor, with an additional man, was sent on his way to the Mandan villages.

Clark and his party were now descending the Big Horn River. On an island they found a huge Indian lodge, sixty feet in diameter at the base, built of poles covered with bushes. On the tops of the poles were eagle feathers, and from the center hung a stuffed buffalo skin. This was probably a place for councils.

On July 27 they passed from the Big Horn into the Yellowstone and "took a last look at the Rocky Mountains, which had been constantly in view from the first of May."

As they floated down the discolored waters of the Yellowstone, buffalo appeared in vast numbers. "Such was the multitude of these animals, that, although the river, including an island, over which they passed was a mile in length, the herd stretched as thick as they could swim, completely from one side to the other, and the party was obliged to stop for an hour. They consoled themselves for the delay by killing four of the herd, and then proceeded a distance of forty-five miles on an island, below which two other herds of buffalo, as numerous as the first, soon after crossed the river."

On August 2 Captain Clark notes that "the bear which gave so much trouble on the head of the Missouri, are equally fierce in this quarter. This morning one of them, which was on a sandbar as the boat passed, raised himself on his hind feet, and after looking at the party, plunged in and swam towards them. He was received with three balls in the body; he then turned round and made for the shore."

On August 3 they reached the junction of the Yellowstone and the Missouri, where they had made their camp on April 26, 1805. But swarms of mosquitoes gave them such a reception that they moved their camp farther down the river to await the coming of Captain Lewis. Of Sacajawea's poor little child we read, "The face of the Indian child is considerably puffed up and swollen with the bites of these animals." The men themselves could procure scarcely any sleep. When Clark tried to hunt he could not keep the mosquitoes from the barrel of his rifle long enough to take aim.

Sergeant Pryor's adventures with the horses were most trying. At the outset, as we saw, he lost some and had much difficulty in managing the others. He and his companions overtook Clark on August 8, but they had no horses at all. They could only report that the horses had disappeared in the night. All that they were able to find were the tracks of the Indians who had stolen them.

But Pryor's troubles did not end here. "On the following night a wolf bit him through the hand as he lay asleep, and made an attempt to seize Windsor, when Shannon discovered and shot him."

The ingenuity of these men was equal to the emergency. When the horses disappeared, they imitated the Mandans by making boats of buffalo skins stretched around hoops and ribbed with sticks, and in these frail vessels they floated safely down the river until they overtook Captain Clark.

On August 11 Clark encountered two white fur traders from the country of the Illinois, and from these adventurers they gathered some news of the lower country. The fur traders and trappers were always among the first pioneers and explorers of the far West.

On August 12 they were overtaken by the boats commanded by Captain Lewis, who was lying wounded in the pirogue.

The party was now reunited, and they started again on their way to the villages of the Minnetarees and the Mandans.

CHAPTER XIX

ON THE WAY HOME

At the Mandan villages again. Big White accompanies the explorers. Colter remains in the wilderness. His subsequent discovery of the Yellowstone Park. Parting with the faithful squaw. Descending the river. The arrival at St. Louis. The news in Washington. The later life of Lewis and Clark.

Since it was near the Mandan villages that the explorers had passed their first winter, they felt comparatively at home. But they learned that their constant admonitions to keep the peace had not been followed by the neighbors of the Mandans, the Minnetarees, who also were asked to a grand council. There had been fights with Arikaras and Sioux, and the explorers were obliged to try the part of peacemakers again.

One of the main objects of the council was to persuade some chiefs to accompany the explorers to Washington to see the Great

Father, as they called the President. This was very desirable, because the sight of the white people and their cities would impress the Indians and tend to make them more docile. But the Minnetaree chief excused himself on the plea that he was afraid of being killed by the Sioux, which was simply a pretext to avoid a journey that he did not care to make. The Indians were probably suspicious and preferred their own life to that of the white men. But at last Shahakas (Big White), a Mandan chief, agreed to go to Washington.[1]

[1]Lewis and Clark promised Big White a safe return, and he did return finally, after some curious adventures described in Chittenden's "History of the American Fur Trade." In 1807, after his visit to Washington, an expedition was organized at St. Louis to escort Big White, his interpreter, their wives and two children, back to the Mandan villages. It was commanded by Pryor, who had been promoted to the rank of ensign for his services in the Lewis and Clark expedition. Evidently his loss of the horses was not charged against him. But when the party reached the Arikaras, these Indians demanded goods, and also the surrender of Big White. Pryor refused to give him up. A battle followed and several were killed and wounded on each side. The party were finally obliged to return, and Big White was carried back to St. Louis. In 1809 Captain

A Mandan Chief

The party were now well on their way
home, but the fascination of the wilderness
was so strong that one of the men, John
Colter, a most skillful hunter, applied for per-
mission to leave the expedition and join some
trappers who were going up the river. He
had been away many years from the frontiers,
but just as he was approaching civilization he
turned his back upon it, preferring the wild
life of the plains and mountains.[1] His choice

Lewis, then governor of upper Louisiana, or Missouri territory, made a contract in behalf of the United States with
the newly organized Missouri Fur Company for the return
of Big White under pain of forfeiture of three thousand
dollars. This time the effort was successful, and the much-
suffering Big White was restored to his friends and home,
after an absence of three years. For this it was agreed
that the company should receive seven thousand dollars,
which made Big White a costly visitor for the government.

[1]For Colter this was the beginning of years of strange
adventures. In the winter of 1806–1807 he camped in the
valley of the Yellowstone River. When returning in the
spring of 1807 he met a party directed by Manuel Lisa,
the famous fur trader, and turned back to the wilderness a
second time. He was sent on a long and perilous journey
across the Wind River Mountains and the Teton Range to
confer with the Blackfoot nation. But he became involved
in an Indian war and was obliged to fight with the Crows

brought him a permanent place in the history of the West. The next year he became the discoverer of the natural wonders now included in the Yellowstone National Park.

As none of the Minnetarees would accompany the explorers to Washington, Chaboneau the interpreter, with his wife Sacajawea and their child, decided to remain here. "This man has been very serviceable to us," says the

against the Blackfeet. In endeavoring to regain Lisa's party he crossed the Yellowstone National Park alone and saw the geysers. This was a wonderful journey in its extent and its discoveries. The next spring, 1808, he started again for the Blackfeet. His companion was killed. He was captured, stripped naked, and turned loose to run for his life before a multitude of yelling warriors. He ran until the blood burst from his nose and mouth. He outstripped all the Indians save one. That one he killed, and with a last effort ran on to the river, where he dived under fallen logs. There he hid, while the Indians searched above him, "screeching and yelling like so many devils," until at night he swam down the river and made his way naked and half-starved to Lisa's fort. In 1809 he descended the Missouri to St. Louis, three thousand miles alone. He met Clark and aided him in the preparation of his map, upon which Clark traced Colter's route. The last days of the discoverer of the Yellowstone Park were passed peacefully on a farm above La Charette Creek near St. Louis, where he died, probably in 1813.

journal, "and his wife particularly useful among the Shoshonees. Indeed, she has borne with a patience truly admirable the fatigues of so long a route, incumbered with the charge of an infant, who is even now only nineteen months old. We therefore paid him his wages, amounting to five hundred dollars and thirty-three cents, including the price of a horse and a lodge purchased of him." With this we see the last of this devoted and courageous woman.

It was time to start. Big White, unconscious of the many adventures before him, parted with his friends and the weeping squaws. The whole village crowded about the explorers and assured them that they would remember their words and obey the Great Father and keep the peace, except when attacked by the Sioux, and on August 17 they started down the river on the last long stretch of their homeward journey.

These friendly relations offer a sharp contrast to the hostile attitude of the early Spanish explorers in the south.

Presently they met Arikaras and Cheyennes, with whom they held councils, but these were brief for they wished to press on, and on the 25th they made forty-eight miles with the oars. Their meeting with a band of Teton-Sioux was less pacific. These treacherous savages were forbidden to come to the camp, and the men were kept under arms.

When they encountered traders ascending the river they learned news of the civilized world. General James Wilkinson, afterwards notorious from charges of bribery, and of complicity with the treason of which Aaron Burr was accused, had been made governor of Louisiana territory.[1] In the diary of Sergeant Gass there is a reference to the death of Alexander Hamilton, who had been killed by Burr at Weehawken, opposite New York, on July 11, 1804, more than two years before. Nothing could more vividly bring out the long and remote isolation of these explorers than the sergeant's prompt note of this belated

[1]Wilkinson's escapes from convictions by courts-martial failed to clear his character.

piece of news: "Mr. Burr & Genl. Hambleton
fought a Duel, the latter was killed."

After passing the mouth of the Platte they
encountered Gravelines, the interpreter whom
they had sent from Fort Mandan in 1805 to
convey an Arikara chief (who died in Washington), their reports, and some specimens of
natural history to the capital.

On they went, passing through the country of the Kansas Indians without any of the
hostilities which they were prepared to meet.
They encountered more traders and learned
that the general opinion in the United States
was that they were lost. Even in this last
stretch of the long journey they suffered from
scanty supplies, and the journal notes the
gathering of pawpaw fruit for food.

On the 20th, near the mouth of the Gascon-
ade, above St. Louis, they saw some cows
feeding, "and the whole party almost invol-
untarily raised a shout of joy at seeing this
image of civilization and domestic life."

At the French village of La Charette the
inhabitants and traders "were all equally

surprised and pleased at our arrival, for they had long since abandoned all hopes of ever seeing us return."

On the 21st the village of St. Charles turned out to welcome them. The next day they passed with an encampment of troops at Coldwater Creek, and then, on "Tuesday [September] 23, descended the Mississippi and round to St. Louis, where we arrived at twelve o'clock, and having fired a salute went on shore and received the heartiest and most hospitable welcome from the whole village."

They had successfully completed the greatest of American explorations, a wilderness journey covering eight thousand miles and lasting for two years and four months.[1]

[1]Great as this journey was, it has sometimes been subject to misconceptions. "First across the Continent" is the title chosen by Mr. Noah Brooks for his narrative of Lewis and Clark. They were not the first. Cabeza de Vaca crossed the continent on the south nearly three hundred years before. Coronado and De Soto between them practically traversed the continent. Of the explorers in British North America on the north, two are preëminent, Samuel Hearne and Alexander Mackenzie. In 1771–1772 Hearne gained the distinction of being the first white man to reach

Captain Lewis at once sent letters to President Jefferson announcing his return, which took nearly a month to reach Washington. Jefferson's reply, dated October 20, expressed his "unspeakable joy" at the news, the first that had reached him since Gravelines brought their message from the Mandan villages in 1805.

Early in 1807 the two leaders went to Washington, where they met with a most enthusiastic reception. Congress voted fifteen hundred acres of public land to Lewis and a thousand to Clark. It is characteristic that Lewis did not wish to receive more land than Clark. The officers were voted double pay, and each of the other members

Lake Athabasca and the Coppermine River, which he followed to the Arctic Ocean. He proved that the belief in a northwest passage from Hudson Bay to the Pacific was unfounded, although the tradition lingered even after his journey. In 1793 a more famous explorer, Alexander Mackenzie, made a successful expedition westward from Lake Athabasca. He passed through the mountains and descended the Fraser River in British Columbia to the sea. This was the first journey across the continent, with the exception of Cabeza de Vaca's flight far to the south. It might well be called a "Northwest Passage by land," to apply a phrase used by a later traveler.

of the expedition received three hundred acres of land.[1]

In telling the story of this wonderful journey it has not been desirable to give the elaborate results of the minute observations made by the explorers. In addition to the

[1]Captain Lewis was appointed governor of Louisiana territory in 1807 and resigned from the army. Captain Clark was appointed general of the militia of the territory and Indian agent.

The whole Purchase had been divided into the territory of Orleans, representing roughly the present state of Louisiana, and Louisiana territory, which was all the rest north of the state.

Captain Lewis's end was a sad one. On a journey to Washington in 1809 he stayed for the night at a rough wayside inn near Memphis, Tennessee. In the morning he was found dead, probably by his own hand, for he was subject to attacks of great depression.

Captain Clark was offered a commission as brigadier general in the War of 1812 with the command held by the unsuccessful General Hull on the northwestern frontier, but he declined to serve. In 1813 President Madison appointed him governor of Missouri territory, as upper Louisiana was then called. He served until Missouri became a state in 1821, when he was a candidate for governor, but was defeated. In 1822 President Monroe made him superintendent of Indian affairs, an office which he filled successfully until his death at St. Louis in 1838.

many notes upon Indians, soil, flora, and fauna
in the narrative, the journals are accompanied
by a long appendix. This contains tables and
notes giving the names and estimated number
of the Indian tribes, daily records of weather
and wind, notes upon the rivers, and careful memoranda regarding soil, vegetation, and
animals. These observations and the careful
surveys and maps testify to the thoroughness
and knowledge with which the explorers did
their work, just as the story which we have
followed shows their ingenuity and perseverance, their tact in dealing with obstacles, and
their courage in the face of danger. The
journey which they made is one of the world's
greatest explorations, and its story has become
a classic among the travel tales of history.

LOUISIANA

===

Part III

THE EXPLORATION OF THE WEST

CHAPTER XX

PIKE'S EXPLORATIONS

Ascending the Mississippi. A second expedition westward. Hostile Spanish influence. Into Colorado. The first glimpse of Pike's Peak. On the upper Arkansas. Disappointment and privation. In Spanish territory. Captured by the Spaniards. Pike's return and death.

While the Lewis and Clark expedition was struggling across the mountains in 1805 another explorer was on his way from St. Louis northward. Lewis and Clark were sent by the President, and theirs was the first governmental exploration of the Louisiana territory. The second exploration was a military one, and was the first military expedition sent into the new country. It was commanded by Lieutenant Zebulon M. Pike, a young army officer, born in Lamberton, New Jersey, in 1779.

In 1805 General James Wilkinson, the commanding officer of the army, ordered Lieutenant

Pike to ascend the Mississippi to its head waters. He was to make the sovereignty of the United States known to the Indians and Canadian traders. He was to observe the country, and to ascertain if possible the sources of the Mississippi.

It was on August 9, 1805, that Lieutenant Pike left St. Louis with twenty men to carry out his orders. They traveled in a keel boat seventy feet long. Provisions for four months were carried, but as it turned out nearly nine months passed before they returned. They ascended the river with few adventures and on September 22 they camped near the site of the present city of St. Paul, where they held a council with the Sioux.

From this point, undeterred by cold and scanty supplies, they made a plucky winter journey to Leech Lake (Minnesota), which Pike supposed, erroneously, to be the main source of the Mississippi. He overlooked the real source, Lake Itasca. They reached Leech Lake on February 1, but after various explorations and some negotiations with the Indians, which included a treaty with the Sioux, they turned back. Of the Falls of St. Anthony, Pike gives a vivid picture, and his journal is full of interest, although less detailed than that of Lewis and Clark. On April 30 the expedition returned to St. Louis. The lieutenant had learned much about the upper river, although he was mistaken as to its source, and his expedition had succeeded in proclaiming the dominion of the United States.

More important and more closely associated with our narrative was Pike's second expedition. In July, 1806, he left St. Louis with a military party numbering twenty-three, under orders from General Wilkinson to travel westward into the interior of Louisiana, to reach the sources of the Arkansas River, and to explore the mountains of the present state of Colorado. He also escorted to their homes fifty-one Osage and Pawnee chiefs and their people who had visited Washington.

The first part of Pike's route was by water up the Missouri, and then up the Osage to the villages of the Osage Indians. Thence he traveled overland through Kansas to a Pawnee village.

The cession of Louisiana with its indefinite boundaries had already caused complications with the Spaniards, who held the southwest, including the present state of Texas. They had heard of Pike's expedition and had sent an armed force to turn him back from any territory which they claimed, or to make him a prisoner. Out of this grew trouble later.

The Spaniards had held a council with the Pawnees and had made them presents of flags. Even after Pike had explained to them the American ownership of the country, and an old Pawnee warrior had obediently brought out a Spanish flag and taking it from its staff replaced it with the American flag, the Pawnee chief tried to keep the Americans from continuing westward, saying that he had promised the Spaniards to intercept them. But Pike kept resolutely on.

As they crossed the plains they saw the old camps of the Spanish troops who had preceded them. Buffalo, wild horses, and prairie dogs furnished variety to the journey, but between the Indians on the one hand and Spaniards on the other the march was not a cheerful one.

They turned southward and reached the Arkansas River near the present town of Great Bend, Kansas. There Pike sent some of his men down the river, while with the others he ascended into Colorado and camped at the site of the later city of Pueblo.

On November 15, while on the Purgatory River and about a week before they reached Pueblo, Pike made the discovery which has served in a sense as his monument. He writes: "I thought I could distinguish a mountain to our right which appeared like a small blue cloud; viewed it with the spy-glass and was still more confirmed in my conjecture; . . . in half an hour they [the mountains] appeared in full view before us. When our small party arrived on the hill they with one accord gave three cheers to the Mexican Mountains."

This was the main range of the Rocky Mountains, and the "blue cloud" is known to this day as Pike's Peak.

On the 24th Pike and a few companions left the camp which they had made at Pueblo, in the hope of climbing the peak. He was not accustomed to mountains like these or to the rarefied air, which makes the distance seem much less. The peak was really fifty miles away in an air line and a hundred by land. They traveled many miles and climbed lower mountain ridges, only to find the summit of the "Grand Peak" still towering distantly above them. What with snow, thin clothing, and scanty food, the party were in a wretched condition, and on the 27th they turned back to the camp. Thus ended the first attempt to climb Pike's Peak.[1]

Continuing their ascent of the Arkansas, the party reached the present site of Cañon City, where the Grand Cañon withheld a passage yielded years later to the railroad.

---

[1] The motto of the later gold seekers in the fifties was "Pike's Peak or Bust." Some of them were forced to change it to "Busted." Pike might have done the same.

Turning aside they ascended Oil Creek to South Park, passed along the South Platte, and, continuing, again reached the Arkansas.

PIKE'S PEAK TRAIL AT MINNEHAHA FALLS

In spite of the bitter cold of a Rocky Mountain winter, Pike ascended the Arkansas to its sources near Leadville, and descended it to Cañon City. This was another disappointment, for he had thought himself on the Red River, whose sources he had been instructed to discover.

On January 14, 1807, notwithstanding the midwinter weather, Pike pluckily started out to find the Red River. He made his way up Grape Creek, which flows into the Arkansas, and through the Wet Mountain valley. Food was scarce. The men were frost-bitten and some of them crippled for life. But they kept on over the Sangre de Cristo Range into the San Luis valley. There he descended the Rio Grande. On reaching the entrance of the Rio Conejos on January 31, he built a stockade and encamped. He was now in southern Colorado, and his search for the Red River had led him into Spanish territory. As a matter of fact this river was really the Canadian, which rises not far from Santa Fé in New Mexico.

Pike himself was carrying out Wilkinson's orders, but just what these orders were is doubtful. Wilkinson was implicated in the plot attributed to Aaron Burr to found a new empire in the valley of the Mississippi.

Zebulon M. Pike

The historian McMaster thinks that Pike was ordered to descend into Mexico as a part of this plot. But Pike himself denied any knowledge of such motives, and it seems certain that whatever Wilkinson's intentions were, Pike was entirely innocent. There is a certain mystery over the reasons for this invasion of Spanish territory.

Whatever the exact facts were, the result was the arrest of Pike and his party on February 26 by a Spanish force. It was done under the guise of a polite invitation to visit the Spanish governor at Santa Fé. Pike was taken into Mexico as a prisoner, but after many journeys he was escorted through Texas and delivered to his countrymen at Natchitoches, Louisiana, on July 1, 1807.

Thus the expedition had an unfortunate ending. But the value of Pike's explorations of the central part of the Purchase will always be an honor to his memory.[1]

---

[1] In the War of 1812 he was made a brigadier general. He died in battle, killed when storming the batteries of York, the capital of Upper Canada.

CHAPTER XXI

ROUTES OF EXPLORATION

The great water ways. Importance of the Missouri. The Santa Fé, Overland, and Oregon trails. The fur trade the chief industry. Its effect on exploration.

After these pioneer American explorations came the extension of the fur trade, the earlier expeditions to Santa Fé, the overland journey to Astoria in 1811–1813, the exploits of leaders like William H. Ashley, and the journeys of Wyeth and others. But before the story of exploration is followed farther it will be helpful to note the beginning of regular routes from the great central valley to the vague confines of Louisiana and beyond to the sea.

Nature did much for the explorers and builders of the West in offering them passage on the great rivers flowing from the mountains to the central valley of the continent. Man, following in the footsteps of buffalo and elk along land routes where nature had smoothed

EMIGRANT TRAIN CROSSING THE PLAINS

the way and cleft the mountains, wore deeper the pathways, which became historic trails.

Sometimes the paths of animals, of hunters, trappers, gold seekers, and emigrants, became the route of the railroad,—a route with an almost forgotten history.

Without the water routes the exploration and later development of the vast interior known as Louisiana would have been a different story. The Great Lakes offered a highway for the French. The Wisconsin River led them to the first explorations of the Mississippi and the discovery that it flowed to the Gulf of Mexico and not to the western sea. In the early Spanish history the navigation of rivers played an insignificant part, but for French explorers, trappers, and traders the water ways were all-important.

East of the Mississippi the Ohio was the greatest of the historic water ways. It was down the Ohio and other tributaries of the Mississippi that there poured the wave of pioneer conquest which was to sweep away any foreign possession of Louisiana.

West of the Mississippi there were the Osage, the Kansas, the Arkansas, the Red

PIKE'S PEAK FROM PIKE'S PEAK AVENUE, COLORADO SPRINGS.

River, and the Platte, all early routes of consequence, and, by far the greatest from every
point of view, there was the Missouri.[1]

The water which has its source at the head
of the Jefferson fork of the Missouri, on the
Rocky Mountain dividing line between Montana and Idaho, reaches the Gulf of Mexico
after a journey of forty-two hundred and
twenty-one miles. The enormous extent of
the Mississippi's drainage basin is illustrated
by the fact that the water which passes
through the great river's mouth to the sea
comes from no fewer than twenty-eight states
and the Indian territory.[2] The Missouri-Mississippi reckoned as a continuous water route
forms the longest river in the world. Its

[1]The mouth of the Missouri was discovered by Marquette and Joliet in 1673. The river was entered about
1700 by the French, who ascended farther and farther,
until Chittenden estimates that by the time St. Louis was
founded in 1764 the river had been explored for a thousand
miles. In 1804 Lewis and Clark had been preceded by
white men almost up to the mouth of the Yellowstone.

[2]Mr. George Cary Eggleston's story, "The Last of the
Flat-boats," gives a suggestive popular sketch of the magni-
tude, political consequence, and peculiarities of this system.

tortuous way, its frequent changes of course, and its destructive floods have presented problems yet unsolved. The time may come when great reservoirs will gather the surplus waters of floods like those of the spring of 1903, but, in spite of the attempts of man, the Missouri remains as unfettered as when Marquette and Joliet shrank appalled from the seething torrent at its mouth. Historically the part of the Missouri has been of the first importance. "For fully a hundred years" (up to about 1875), says Chittenden, "the history of the Missouri River was the history of the country through which it flowed." The explorer, trapper and trader, priest and soldier, prospector, miner, and buffalo hunter, and the military forces of the United States[1] swelled the number

[1]As early as 1819, when the first steamboat entered the Missouri, arrangements were made, but not carried out, for the transportation of troops to the Yellowstone. In 1825 troops were carried in keel boats propelled by wheels turned by hand. After 1855 the steamboat played a large part in military operations along the Missouri and its tributaries. Of the various dramatic incidents of the steamboat days in the remote Northwest, one of the most stirring was the run of the *Far West* after the Custer massacre in

of travelers upon this great water way. The
early nineteenth century brought a new and
most important era in the coming of the steamboat.[1] Another chapter was opened later in
the transportation of troops; and still another
a little later in the northwestern discoveries
of gold.[2] Taking the Missouri-Mississippi as

1876. Down the narrow and unknown Big Horn, down
the dangerous Yellowstone and the Missouri, the *Far
West* was driven with the speed of a railway train, bringing to Bismarck her load of wounded soldiers and the
full reports of the battle—a thousand miles in fifty-four
hours.

In 1877 General Miles's good fortune in finding a steamboat near the mouth of the Muscleshell (Musselshell) enabled him to gain sufficiently on Chief Joseph and the
fleeing Nez Percés, who were nearing British soil, to overtake them within fifty miles of the boundary line.

[1]A steamboat was built at Pittsburg as early as 1811
and descended to New Orleans.

[2]In 1863 came the rich Alder Gulch discovery of gold
placers on a branch of the Jefferson fork of the Missouri,
and the following year the gold of Last Chance Gulch laid
the foundation of the future capital of Montana,—Helena.
The discoveries of mineral wealth which followed were the
beginnings of Montana's prosperity, and one immediate
effect was a vast increase in steamboat traffic. "Prior to
1864," says Chittenden, "there had been only six steamboat arrivals at Fort Benton. In 1866 and 1867 there were

a whole, one may well agree with Chittenden that no river on the continent has an equal record. As for the Mississippi alone, the great central river or trunk line, whose tributaries drain both the Alleghenies and the Rocky Mountains, its commanding position in political as well as economic history is only imperfectly illustrated in Madison's comment in

seventy. The trade touched highwater mark in 1867 and at this time presented one of the most extraordinary developments known to the history of commerce. There were times when thirty or forty steamboats were on the river between Fort Benton and the mouth of the Yellowstone."

But just as the steamboat succeeded the pirogues, or "log dugouts," the "bull boats" of buffalo hide, the mackinaw boats built of planks, and the keel boats worked by oar and sail which formed the representative craft before steam, so the coming of the railroad supplanted the steamboat after a contest which lasted from about 1859, when the railroad reached St. Joseph, Missouri, to about 1887.

To-day there are probably more steamboats on the Yukon River in Alaska than are to be found on the Mississippi above St. Louis, and several times the number of the Missouri River boats, since the Missouri is nearly abandoned. One minor practical outcome of American expansion and development is shown in the fact that many of the pilots and other steamboat men trained on these rivers have been taken to the Yukon, where, it is said, their skill is making serious accidents a thing of the past.

1802, that "The Mississippi is everything to the Western people: the Hudson, the Delaware, the Potomac, and all the navigable streams of the United States formed into one stream." The great steamboat traffic of the Mississippi and its tributaries, which employed four thousand boats in 1850, forms a history distinctive in its methods, its economics, and its picturesqueness.[1]

Even before the great water ways first knew the canoe of the explorer, a Spaniard had made a wonderful land journey which traversed in part a route famous nearly three centuries later as the highway of traders, soldiers, and emigrants. The first association of the Santa Fé trail with white men goes back to the journey of Coronado, but it was not until the early nineteenth century that the path from Independence on the Missouri to Santa Fé,

[1] Mark Twain's "Life on the Mississippi" and his "Roughing It" have a distinct historical value as pictures of the past life of the water ways and the interior of the West. The last stage of the contest between the steamboat and the railroad below St. Louis has been dramatized, as it were, in Mr. G. W. Ogden's novel, "Tennessee Todd."

New Mexico, became a trading route.[1] Originally the way was west by Council Grove and along the Arkansas to Bent's Fort, which was east of La Junta, and thence south, by the Raton Pass, to Santa Fé. Later the river was left at Cimarron Crossing, near Dodge City, and the route traversed the desert in a nearly direct southwesterly line. In the country of the Missouri-Mississippi there were manufactured goods. In the Spanish Southwest there was a waiting and eager market.[2] Thus, before the close of the first

---

[1]For a time Blue Mills, Missouri, was a starting point. The year 1817 brought the first stage of steamboat navigation of the Mississippi, and two years later the first steamboat reached the Missouri. The appearance of the steamboat brought more traffic for the trail. Later, Independence was found a more convenient point of departure.

[2]The first trading expedition from the upper Mississippi country to Santa Fé was about 1760, according to Captain Amos Stoddard's "Sketches of Louisiana," and resulted in the imprisonment of the would-be traders and confiscation of their goods. Under Spanish rule there was some intercourse but no trade of consequence, and the second trading expedition is noted by Chittenden as that of William Morrison of Kaskaskia, Illinois, afterwards a partner of the famous Spanish fur trader, Manuel Lisa. This was in 1807.

quarter of the century, there began that "commerce of the prairie" which made the Santa Fé trail, down to the coming of the railroad, the greatest land trading route of the West. Traversing as the trail did the haunts of the fiercest Indians of the plains,

Pike's journey, and his involuntary journey to Santa Fé, formed the first visit of an officer of our government. Just before Pike the Spaniards had sent an armed force to the Pawnee villages at Kansas to enlist the interest of the Indians against the Americans. There were various minor expeditions over the trail in the first twenty years of the century, including the journeys of A. P. Chouteau and Julius de Munn in 1815–1817; but William Becknell of Missouri, "the father of the Santa Fé trail," is credited by Chittenden with the founding of this route commercially. Inman gives the date of his first expedition as 1812, but this should probably be later. The earlier traders had caravans of horses and mules. Wheeled vehicles were introduced probably about 1825, and Becknell was the first to take wagons over the trail. In that day cheap domestic cotton cloths could be sold for over two dollars a yard in Santa Fé. The possibilities of trade with New Mexico were seen by Senator Thomas Hart Benton of Missouri, "the father of the West," who introduced a bill in 1824, which became a law, for the survey of a route from the Missouri to New Mexico. But the survey was imperfectly carried out and the traders followed the old wagon route, portions of which are now followed by the main line of the Atchison, Topeka, and Santa Fé Railroad.

commerce was forced to fight its way. The Santa Fé trail was the first great plains route for the interchange of trade between white men. Its history began with the Spaniards. It was a history of traffic rather than of emigrant travel, but a history second to none in its record of peril and adventure.[1]

The Oregon as well as the Santa Fé trail had its real beginning at Independence, Missouri. From St. Louis the journey was by water. The overland traffic, when the river was left behind for the journey across the plains, led to the foundation of Independence, Missouri,—which preserves its identity,—and Westport, afterwards absorbed into Kansas City which was laid out in 1838. Forty-one miles west from Independence the two trails parted company, and there for a time stood a sign announcing the great journey before the traveler in the simple words, "Road to Oregon." To the northwest the "road"

[1]The romance and adventure of this picturesque old trail is well illustrated in Colonel Henry Inman's "The Old Santa Fé Trail." Unfortunately the author's history is not reliable.

stretched away to the Columbia, a distance of two thousand miles.[1] The Oregon trail was

[1]The trail crossed the Kansas River near the city of Topeka, reached the Platte River in Nebraska, and followed up the Platte along the south and then the north fork to Fort Laramie, which was a station much in use for rest and repairs, since there was no other similar halting place until Fort Bridger was reached, three hundred and ninety-four miles beyond. The trail continued along the North Platte, which was forded near Caspar, Wyoming, but was left behind a few miles farther on, since the trail continued westward, passing a famous landmark near the valley of the Sweetwater which was named Independence Rock, probably by Ashley, before 1830. From the Devil's Gate, a remarkable cañon through which the Sweetwater flows, the trail went on to the great South Pass in Wyoming, between the Wind River Mountains and the Sweetwater Range. The first discovery of this pass was due not to Hunt and the Astorians of 1811–1813, but, in Chittenden's opinion, to one of the parties of the fur trader and explorer, Alexander Henry, in 1823. At Fort Bridger, built in 1843 by the famous trapper, explorer, and guide, James Bridger, who discovered Great Salt Lake, the traveler had journeyed over a thousand miles. The trail kept on in a northwesterly direction, passing Fort Hall on the Snake River, and Fort Boise, and near Pendleton reaching the Umatilla River, which was followed to the Columbia, eighteen hundred and thirty-five miles from Independence. Two hundred miles down the Columbia the end of the trail was reached at Fort Vancouver, opposite the mouth of the Willamette.

of peculiar consequence from its relation not only to trade but also to the settlement of the country beyond the mountains, a country which could not have been settled by Americans without the control of land routes made possible by the acquisition of Louisiana.

Another of the great routes which was partly identical with the Oregon trail ran directly westward,—the Overland trail, as it came to be known, from St. Joseph, Missouri, and also from Council Bluffs along the Platte to Fort Laramie and westward. This route left the Oregon trail near Fort Hall, and crossed the desert to the Truckee River and California.[1] This was the main route of the overland gold seekers and emigrants in '49 and subsequent years. To the south there

[1] The trail turned south and west beyond Fort Bridger, and the usual route was known as the Salt Lake Trail, which is described by Colonel Henry Inman in his picturesque though not infallible volume, "The Great Salt Lake Trail." There were at least three other early trails of considerable but lesser consequence. The exact identification of these routes is difficult, but Chittenden's itineraries are recommended for consultation.

was, later in the century, a mail route from
Fort Smith, Arkansas, southwest through
Texas and west to California.

Three great land routes and one vast water
way are to be remembered as the most potent
earlier means of traversing Louisiana, developing its trade and reaching the country
beyond the mountains. On the maps of
to-day, while the routes are identical only in
part, we find the Santa Fé trail succeeded by
the Atchison, Topeka, and Santa Fé Railroad,
the Oregon trail by the Oregon Short Line
and other railroads, and the Overland trail by
the Union and Central Pacific.

Greatest of all industries in the early history of Louisiana was the trade in furs,
which centered in St. Louis. It was a traffic
inherited from the French, who were far more
active in its development than the Spaniards,
although certain of the latter, like Manuel Lisa,
were traders of renown. The mineral wealth
of the mountains lay unrevealed for nearly
half a century after American occupation.
Agriculture, save within easy distance of the

lower Missouri, expanded but little until after
the Civil War. A complete history of upper
Louisiana to 1843, when emigration to the
West began, would be in larger part a history of the fur trade. In 1847 it was estimated that the annual value of the St. Louis
fur trade for the preceding forty years had
been between two hundred and three hundred
thousand dollars. The conduct of the trade
from 1806 to 1843 in a country swarming
with hostile Indians is estimated[1] to have
cost the lives of three hundred traders and
the destruction of property valued at over
two hundred thousand dollars.

The management of the business was not
a question of individuals or firms, but of
great companies and of combinations. In
the north there had been early exemplars.
In Canada there was the far-reaching Hudson
Bay Company, organized in 1670 with the
picturesque adventurer, Pierre Radisson, as
its originator, and Prince Rupert at its head,
and there was also its sometime rival, the

[1]Chittenden.

Northwest Fur Company. The Mackinaw Company had the trade of the Great Lakes. From the time of the Louisiana cession to 1845, St. Louis was the headquarters of the fur trade of the far West and the home of various companies with longer or shorter careers—the American, Rocky Mountain, Missouri, and companies and firms whose rivalry in the field, like the hostility of the Hudson Bay and Northwest companies in the North, added some dark pages to the frontier history of the continent. In the Northwest, John Jacob Astor, seeing the possibilities of the fur trade, founded Astoria at the mouth of the Columbia in 1811—an unsuccessful experiment—and began an effort to reorganize and combine the fur trade.

At once this commercial activity quickened the exploration of the interior. The trappers sent from St. Louis ascended the Osage and Kansas rivers, and the Platte, or went southward along the Arkansas. The Missouri became the great thoroughfare for the traders and trappers passing to and from the streams issuing from the distant mountains. The *bourgeois* or manager, the clerk, the hunter and trapper, camp-keeper, *voyageur* or boatman, the novices or "pork eaters," and the artisans represented the various grades enrolled on the books of the old fur companies. They were the regular army of the wilderness traffic, and in addition there were the soldiers of fortune, or free trappers, who scorned allegiance to any standard save their own. "Gamesters of the Wilderness"[1] were these adventurers, staking their lives against Indians or rivals as freely as they staked their earnings when they returned to St. Louis after months or perhaps years of savage isolation. They were not without reproach, but of fear they knew nothing. Theirs was the work of pioneers and pathfinders, not in the cause of settlement and possession, but for the sake of the commerce afforded by the wild things of the streams and forests. There were the buffalo hunters also, slaughtering for hides

[1] An apt title given by Miss A. C. Laut in her vivid narrative, "The Story of the Trapper."

alone, and at their door is to be laid the larger responsibility for the massacres which have swept the buffalo from the plains in a generation. But these butchers were a race apart from the earlier trappers. The history of the American fur trade holds names like those of Chouteau, Lisa, Ashley, Sublette, Vanderburgh, and Bridger, which are of large significance in the early history of the West. Nor is theirs simply a saga of brave deeds, of wild adventure and wilder license, since the part which they played in the exploration of the West was of immediate and lasting consequence.

CHAPTER XXII

TYPICAL PATHFINDERS

Trade seeking the Northwest. Hunt and the "overland Astorians." Ashley and Wyeth. Bonneville's journeys. Explorations by Frémont.

Of the many adventurous journeys to the vague western boundaries of Louisiana and beyond, the most remarkable for the first decade of the American fur trade was the expedition of Wilson Price Hunt, leader of the "overland Astorians." This expedition was due to the commercial enterprise of John Jacob Astor. The journey of Lewis and Clark had shown that the upper Missouri and the country beyond the mountains was rich in furs. Mr. Astor saw a tempting opportunity for trading posts from the mouth of the Columbia to its source and along the Missouri, an opportunity which offered not only trade

226

with our East but a most profitable commerce with China and Japan. In a word, this German "captain of industry" saw a practicable northwest passage, a—possible means of reaching that rich Oriental trade which had tempted the voyages of Columbus and of later seekers for a route to the Spice Islands and Cathay.

In 1808 Mr. Astor organized the American Fur Company, and later the Pacific Fur Company, the latter merely a name for the branch of the first company which was to operate on the Pacific coast. Two expeditions were planned, one to go by sea and one by land. The ship carrying the former left New York in 1810, reaching the mouth of the Columbia the following spring. The foundation of Astoria[1] was accomplished under unfortunate auspices, and the result was a failure that need not be dwelt upon, since our present concern

[1]Washington Irving's classic "Astoria" needs no recommendation. Chittenden, "History of the American Fur Trade," Vol. I, chap. xiv, furnishes some judicial comments upon Irving's accuracy and answers the criticisms of H. H. Bancroft.

lies with Hunt's overland journey, which may be said to have opened the Oregon trail.

In March, 1811, Hunt left St. Louis with his party and ascended the Missouri. His original purpose was to continue up the Missouri and the Yellowstone. But tidings of hostile Blackfeet on the route induced him to leave the river at the country of the Arikaras, thirteen hundred and twenty-five miles above the mouth of the Missouri, and to make the journey by land. His party, sixty-four in number, turned westward into an unknown country. They passed near the Black Hills, and made their way through the Big Horn and Wind River mountains to the valley of Green River. Thence they crossed the divide to the Snake River, and after many bitter experiences in the mountain winter they reached the Columbia late in January, 1812, and on February 15 arrived at Astoria.

This journey occupied three hundred and forty days, and the distance according to Hunt's estimate was thirty-five hundred miles. That summer there was sent back from Astoria a party which, owing to various blunders, spent nearly as long a time on its return journey, so that it was nearly two years before news of Hunt reached St. Louis. These two expeditions showed the way to Oregon. But various mistakes in management, the war with Great Britain, and the approach of an English war vessel resulted in the abandonment of Astoria and the end of Mr. Astor's dream of a northwest trading route to the Orient.[1]

The character of the men who were the first to learn the secrets of the Louisiana wilderness is illustrated in the experiences of General William H. Ashley. A Virginian by birth, he was elected lieutenant governor of Missouri in 1820, but for a time fortune seemed to forsake him. He was the head of the Rocky Mountain Fur Company, but in his first expedition he lost a keel boat and cargo of furs valued at ten thousand dollars. In 1823 his men were overwhelmed by hostile Arikaras,

[1]Perhaps Mr. J. J. Hill, the father of the Great Northern Railroad, has come nearer the realization of the dream than any of Mr. Astor's successors.

and in 1824 he was defeated for governor of Missouri. But in the end the indomitable will which conquered the West for Americans brought him substantial results as explorer and trader. He planned and led expeditions into the interior. Once he journeyed to the mouth of the Yellowstone, and again to the country of the Arikaras. In 1824 he led his men to the Green River valley, in 1825 to Great Salt Lake, and the following year he made his way again to the mountains. His adventurous career and romantic journeys have invested his name with a peculiar distinction in the early history of Missouri.

Among the premature prophets of the greatness of the West was one Hall J. Kelley, a Boston school teacher, who began to preach the rich opportunities of Oregon as early as 1815. Through his influence Nathaniel J. Wyeth of Cambridge learned the fascination of the vaguely known West, and presently there came to him an idea not unlike the Astor plan for a trading company on the Columbia. After various difficulties he organized an expedition and started from St. Louis in 1832, under the guidance of the famous fur traders, the Sublettes. They crossed the plains to Pierre's Hole, now Teton Basin in Idaho, and journeyed on to Fort Walla Walla in Washington, reaching Fort Vancouver near the mouth of the Columbia on October 29. Wyeth returned to the East and in 1834 led a second expedition across the plains and mountains to Oregon. So far as commercial results were concerned, Wyeth's efforts met with failure. But his journeys, remarkable in themselves, are worth citing to illustrate not only the courage and the spirit of adventure which impelled these explorers and traders, but also because Wyeth attracted public attention to the overland route to Oregon and aided in its early occupation by Americans.[1]

In spite of their careful notes on fauna and flora and meteorological and other phenomena,

[1]Wyeth's first expedition was described by the ornithologist, J. K. Townsend, who accompanied him with the botanist, Thomas Nuttall. In 1898 Wyeth's own letters and journals were published by the Oregon Historical Society, edited by Professor F. G. Young.

Lewis and Clark were not professional scientists, but scientific explorers were in the vanguard of Western discovery. As early as 1809–1811, John Bradbury, an English naturalist, traveled up the Mississippi and the Missouri, frequently risking his life in his search for specimens. Bradbury, Thomas Nuttall, J. K. Townsend, an ornithologist, and H. M. Brackenridge were with Hunt and Lisa before the former left the Missouri for his overland journey, and they published the results of their studies. The famous painter and student of Indians, George Catlin, ascended the Missouri in 1832, and painted many portraits of Indians which are preserved in the United States National Museum at Washington. In 1833 Maximilian, Prince of Wied, traveled up the Missouri and spent a winter in the Northwest. His book, "Travels in the Interior of North America," remains the most elaborate work published upon this section of the West. Another scientific explorer was J. N. Nicollet, whose studies in the far West between 1836 and 1840 have a permanent value.

The explorations of Captain Bonneville, U.S.A., from 1832 to 1835, owe much to the genius of Washington Irving. Bonneville had obtained leave from the War Department to make the journey at his own expense, in order to observe the country and the people. He himself seems to have thought more of the possibilities of trade.

He ascended the Platte to Green River, following the usual route of the trappers, and made a camp on Green River, west of South Pass, but his trapping was a failure. He sent out an expedition, which was the second party of American trappers to cross from the neighborhood of Great Salt Lake to California. Bonneville himself, after much journeying in the mountains, crossed into Oregon, but the Hudson Bay Company controlled the trade. After another winter in the mountains he returned in the summer of 1835.

Bonneville's long stay in the mountains yielded scanty results. He made a map of the head waters of the Missouri, Yellowstone, Snake, and other rivers and the country around

Great Salt Lake, and another map of the country westward to the Pacific. In many of their features, however, Gallatin had anticipated him. Captain Chittenden credits Bonneville with the discovery of Humboldt River and lakes, the location of San Joaquin River, California, and the mapping out of the country around the sources of the Big Horn and Green rivers. He was the first to take wagons through South Pass to Green River. But, through his meeting with Washington Irving, Bonneville was enabled to be more useful to literature than to science or commerce.

Although the government was prompt in organizing the first exploration of the Louisiana territory under Lewis and Clark, and another under Pike, it was not until 1842 that official explorations were resumed. Lieutenant J. C. Frémont, U.S.A., who had already traveled with Nicollet in the West, was commissioned to explore the mountains. Most of his work lay to the westward of the Louisiana Purchase, but it is inseparably connected with it, since his object was largely to find the best routes from Louisiana territory westward through the mountains. In June, 1842, he started from the mouth of the Kansas River and made his way up the Platte, through a country alive with hostile Indians, to the South Pass. He explored the Wind River Mountains, and the highest bears his name.

In 1843 he led a second expedition to the heart of the mountains. He found the head waters of the Colorado, reached Salt Lake, and ascended to the Columbia. He returned through the mountains in winter, and after many hardships led his exhausted followers west to Sutter's Fort on the Sacramento in California. In the spring he returned through the mountains.

In 1845–1846 he made another journey through the midst of the Rockies. At this time there was trouble with the Mexicans, who held California. Congress, on May 13, 1846, had declared that war with Mexico existed, but long before government troops reached California, Frémont led the settlers in an uprising which resulted in the freedom of northern California. Frémont was elected governor. His troubles with General Kearny, who commanded the American troops, his arrest, and his enthusiastic reception on his return east form no part of this history. Subsequently he led two more expeditions, one in 1848 along the upper Rio Grande in a finally successful effort to find a route to California, and another in 1853, when he crossed the continent, finding passes through the mountains on the lines of latitude 38° and 39°.

The glamour of Frémont's "pathfinding," which brought him the first Republican nomination for the presidency in 1856, has not sustained the more critical examination of later years. In some of his discoveries Frémont had been anticipated, but the knowledge of passes and mountain routes which he in a sense popularized has proved of value in many different ways. Aside from this and the fact that he really explored much new territory, the courage, endurance, and on the whole the good management shown in his various expeditions are sufficient to make them memorable in Western annals.

After Frémont came an era of government explorations, reconnaissances, and surveys which established routes, indicated the lines of future railroads, and chose the sites of the forts—the frontier posts of order and of law. The West was becoming better known, but before Frémont there was a literature of Western exploration, English and American, which may be roughly described as beginning with Jonathan Carver's "Travels," published in 1778. This curious literature[1] was rare and fragmentary before the Biddle

[1]In 1823 John D. Hunter published in Philadelphia his "Manners and Customs of Several Indian Tribes located West of the Mississippi." The author was a captive among the Kickapoos, and claimed to have crossed the continent with some Osage Indians and to have seen the Pacific. Samuel Parker's "Journal of an Exploring Tour across the Rocky Mountains" appeared in 1838. Wyeth's Memoir was included in Cushing's Report in 1839. J. K. Townsend's "Narrative of a Journey across the Rocky Mountains" was published in 1839. Farnham's well-known "Travels in the Great Western Prairies," etc., was issued in 1843, and was followed in 1849 by G. F. Ruxton's "Life in the Far West." The early memoirs of travelers and hunters, the tales of Indians, the various personal narratives, and the

edition of Lewis and Clark and the meetings
of Bradbury and Brackenridge upon the first
stages of the overland Astorian expedition,
but it expanded to considerable proportions
later. All these additions to knowledge of the
West stimulated curiosity in the older states.

recollections of Colonel R. B. Marcy and other army officers
afford an inviting field for the curious. Among the number may be cited Jacob Fowler's "Journal," relating this
surveyor's journey to the sources of the Rio Grande and
his varied adventures in 1821–1822; Josiah Gregg's "Commerce of the Prairies," an account of the Santa Fé trail,
published in 1844; Charles Larpenteur's "Forty Years a Fur
Trader" (1838–1872); and Father Pierre Jean de Smet's
"Oregon Missions" (1847). The library of the Wisconsin
State Historical Society, the Mercantile Library in St. Louis,
the Lenox Library (now a branch of the New York Public
Library), and certain private libraries like those of Edward
E. Ayer of Chicago, H. H. Bancroft of San Francisco, and
the Hon. Peter Koch of Bozeman, Montana, are rich in
examples of this early literature. The introduction to
"Tales of an Indian Camp," published in London in 1829,
offers this quaint passage: "In the year 1695 a number of
savants associated in Paris for the purpose of procuring
information regarding the Western Indians. They were
called shortly 'The Theoretical and Speculative Society of
Paris,' but their title at large was 'The Society for prose-
cuting Researches in the Western Hemisphere and for procuring Speculations to be made and History drawn up of
the Origin and History of the Ancient and Present Inhabitants.' Madame Maintenon became a member, forbidding,
however, the Society to speculate upon her affairs."

LOUISIANA

═══════

Part IV

THE BUILDING OF THE WEST

CHAPTER XXIII

A FORMATIVE PERIOD

Influences of the westward movement. A time of expansion.
Development of the Mississippi Valley. Influences upon
upper Louisiana. Types of the middle period. The soldier's
work in the West. Labors of missionaries. Whitman's
journey and its real purpose.

In the era of exploration, which may be
roughly defined as the first half of the last century, the interior commerce of upper Louisiana
was represented for the most part by the wares
of trappers and by the traders of the Santa
Fé trail.

But the history of the West was unfolding
rapidly. In the lower country there were the
increasing settlement and business interests
of the state of Louisiana,[1] admitted in 1812,

[1]The picturesque history of Louisiana may be gathered
from a study of B. F. French's "Historical Collections of
Louisiana" and Gayarre's "History of Louisiana." More

of the Southern territories to the east of the
Mississippi, and of Arkansas, which became
a territory in 1819. East of the great river
the pressure of settlement was increased by
the European immigration which followed the
close of the Napoleonic wars. There were foreign as well as domestic reasons for the fact
that the population of Ohio increased from
230,760 to 581,295 between 1810 and 1820,
and that of Indiana from 24,520 to 197,198.

By 1820 eight states had been formed in
the Mississippi valley and the center of population had moved from a point east of Balti-
more in 1789 over a hundred and twenty miles
westward. The commerce of the Ohio and the
lower Mississippi was quickened not only by
the productiveness of new settlers but also
and immeasurably by the introduction and
rapid expansion of steamboat transportation.

The influence of the steamboat is emphasized in the history of St. Louis. In 1800,
nearly forty years after its foundation, the

popular and more accessible are the writings of G. W.
Cable, Miss Grace King, and the references in McMaster.

population was only 925. Hardly more than a thousand residents were to be credited to St. Louis in the year of the Louisiana Purchase. In 1810 it was a village of only 1400 souls. But in 1817 the first steamboat reached St. Louis and marked the opening of a traffic imperial in its range. From the upper navigable waters of the Mississippi and Missouri, from the Ohio and the Illinois, and from New Orleans, the steamboat brought the trade of the vast region bounded by the Alleghenies and Rocky Mountains, and in addition the commerce of the eastern seaboard and traffic with foreign countries found their way up the Mississippi and centered in St. Louis. With such a history it is inevitable that the possibility of sending the modern traffic of the West by water to the sea, and reopening the once vigorous life of this great water way, should be a subject of perennial interest. A century after the Louisiana Purchase finds the West concerned with the possibilities of various canal routes, the improvement of river navigation, and the possibilities of deep-sea traffic direct to St. Louis, while the East, so far as New York may be held representative, has been debating the value of an improved Erie Canal in holding the commerce of the West. History repeats itself, but there is no repetition of the argument of Eastern Federalists that the purchase of Louisiana was a waste of money upon a profitless wilderness.

On the North and East in the early years of the last century there were multiplying factors of growth. The War of 1812 settled finally the ownership of the whole "Old Northwest," comprising Ohio, Indiana, Illinois, Michigan, Wisconsin, and a portion of Minnesota. The swift growth of this great section swelled the commerce of the river, although the completion of the Erie Canal in 1825 gave the Northwest an outlet directly east.

In the South the introduction of the cotton gin stimulated a movement of Southern planters toward virgin fields farther west. In the Southwest there developed the stormy early history of Texas, with its American invasion and possession, and its admission as a state in 1845. From the British possessions to the Gulf the American pressure westward was everywhere in evidence.

The movement of pioneer settlers across the plains to Oregon, whose definition and possession afforded so acute an issue between the United States and Great Britain,[1] began in the thirties. In 1846 came our war with Mexico and another expansion westward which included the distant Southwest and California, the goal of treasure seekers during the years following 1848.

Many of the conditions and changes sketched so summarily affected the old Louisiana territory only indirectly so far as settlement was concerned, save for the growth of the states of Louisiana and Missouri and of Arkansas. The interior of the Louisiana Purchase was occupied more slowly, but from the date of acquisition the cities of New Orleans and

[1]The rival claims of England and America to Oregon in 1845–1846 gave rise to the historic watchword "Fifty-four forty or fight," but this line was sensibly abandoned in favor of a compromise on the line of 49°—a continuation of the dividing line east of the mountains.

St. Louis showed a swiftly increasing commercial consequence. The tide of settlement
overleapt the Missouri-Mississippi and showed
itself in eastern Kansas in the thirties. Of
this settlement and its later political relations
something remains to be said in another
chapter. The purpose of this rapid summary
is merely to indicate the general conditions
surrounding the formative period of the old
Louisiana Purchase.

Throughout all the changing scenes of our
early Western history one figure remains constant—the American regular soldier, whose
close relation to Louisiana began with the expedition of Lewis and Clark. From that time to
the last of our Indian campaigns, the unfortunate trouble with the Sioux at Wounded Knee
in 1890, the soldier has done heroic work in the
building and safeguarding of the West. He
has watched over wagon trains and railroad
builders, protected settlers, and faced every
form of danger, under the burning sun of Texas
deserts and the icy skies of mountain winters,
for the preservation of order, law, and life.

The military history opened by Lewis and Clark was continuous. St. Louis was an early headquarters. There was an attempt to send troops up the Missouri in 1819. Fort Leavenworth was made a military post in 1832, and as the overland travel grew, a line of forts was established which began with Fort Kearny at Grand Island on the Platte, three hundred miles northwest of Fort Leavenworth, and was continued with Fort Laramie in Wyoming, Fort Bridger and Fort Hall in Idaho, —the latter at the entrance to the Oregon country,—and other forts. Out of this line of posts grew the system of old forts, each with a moving history, that formerly dotted the entire West.

The English soldier has received a meed of recognition for his deeds which to the American regular is practically unknown. From the time of the American Revolution a republic's jealousy of a professional soldiery has inured to the disadvantage of the gallant men who have had so large a part in the westward advance of the American frontier. What their purely military part has been in this work beyond the Missouri can be inferred from a few illustrations. A journey of a thousand miles from his base of supplies into a hostile country was the record of Colonel Kearny of the First Dragoons, who on the breaking out of the war with Mexico in 1846 marched from Fort Leavenworth to Santa Fé with seventeen hundred men and seized the town. "A little later he pushed on to California with three hundred wilderness-worn dragoons in shabby and patched clothing who had long been on a short allowance of food." After him Colonel St. George Cooke led the half-starved volunteers of the Mormon Battalion, who after infinite hardships opened a wagon road to California.

The Utah expedition of 1857 from Fort Leavenworth against the Mormons proved fruitless, but the splendid endurance of starvation and the rigors of a Rocky Mountain winter showed the mettle of the American soldier.

The Indian wars which accompanied and followed the building of the Union Pacific and the slaughter of the buffalo furnished years of active army life. In 1866 Colonel Carrington defied the Sioux and built, in the north near the Big Horn Mountains, a new fort—Phil. Kearny—an outpost of civilization. His march and the building of the fort were accompanied by ceaseless attacks from the Sioux. The fort was finished, but it was assailed again and again. The massacre of Colonel Fetterman, Captain Brown, and sixty-five men was one of the bloody episodes. But the next year Captain James Powell with some thirty men repulsed probably three thousand Indians, who then learned for the first time the murderous effect of breech-loading rifles.

In 1868 General G. A. Forsyth held a sand-bar on the Republican River in Kansas against perhaps one thousand Indians—his command numbering originally fifty men. It was not until the eighth day that relief came to the remnant of this gallant band. Custer's campaign against Black Kettle in the bitter winter of 1868, Crook's conquest of the Apaches in 1871 and 1872, the Sioux campaigns of 1876 and the Custer massacre, the pursuit of Chief Joseph and the Nez Percés, covering some fourteen hundred miles through Idaho, Wyoming, and Montana to Dakota, and the Apache campaigns of 1881–1883, are only a few examples of the active service of the soldier in the West.[1]

Like the soldier, the missionary was an early figure in the history of the West. Fray Juan de Padilla, who yielded his life on the plains of Kansas after Coronado's return, was the first of a long line of heroic priests and Protestant missionaries who accompanied, or followed close behind, the Western pioneers. Their first field within the Louisiana Purchase lay in the lower country and along the eastern borders. A full history of their work, which will never be written, would afford many inspiring and touching pages.

Among the Roman Catholic missionaries the most conspicuous figure is Father Pierre

[1] "The Story of the Soldier," by General G. A. Forsyth, furnishes a needed picture of the work done in the West.

Jean de Smet. Between 1820 and 1830 he was engaged in mission work in lower Louisiana. In 1838 he went northward to minister to the Pottawattomie Indians near Council Bluffs, but in 1840 he was sent to the Flathead Indians of the Northwest. His life among them and his frequent journeys up and down the western country have fortunately been preserved in his letters, which form a most valuable record of his period.

The early thirties witnessed the beginning of the Oregon missions, which were the first Protestant efforts in the interior. A Methodist delegation under Jason and Daniel Lee accompanied Wyeth as far as Snake River in 1834, and continued on alone to found missions in Oregon. In 1835 Dr. Marcus Whitman of Wheeler, New York, and the Rev. Samuel Parker were first sent out by the American Board of Commissioners for Foreign Missions. Missions were ultimately established at Waiilatpu[1] and elsewhere. In the winter of 1843 Dr. Whitman made a remarkable journey from

[1]Now Walla Walla, Washington.

Waiilatpu down the mountains to Taos, New Mexico, and thence to St. Louis and eastward. This journey has been the subject of an unfortunately bitter discussion. It has been claimed

WHITMAN'S JOURNEY TO SAVE HIS MISSION

that Whitman made this journey to present the case of Oregon as against the claims of Great Britain in the dispute over the northern boundary, and that by efforts at Washington and by gathering emigrants he saved Oregon to the United States. The whole matter has been subjected to close analysis in recent years, and it may be accepted that Whitman's journey east was primarily for the purpose of preserving his mission, which the Board had intended to close, and that he exercised no political influence. It is obvious, of course, that he desired to increase American immigration, but his practical results in this direction were limited. Of his bravery his journey gave sufficient proof, and his devotion to his work was sealed by his death at the hands of Indians in 1847.[1]

In view of the adventurous character of "Whitman's ride," it is not strange that it

[1] The legend of Whitman as "the savior of Oregon" assumed tangible form some years after his death, and was first made public by a former colleague in 1864. The popularity of the legend may be said to date from 1882–1883, and particularly from the publication of "Oregon: The Struggle for Possession," by the Rev. William Barrows. In spite of H. H. Bancroft's carefully verified narrative of the facts, published about the same time, the legend obtained acceptance not only in popular literature but also in school histories and encyclopedias. The output

became invested with a romantic interest which Whitman himself would probably have disclaimed in large measure could he have lived to see some of the later literature upon his journey.

of books and periodical literature upon the subject has developed to surprising proportions and involves a controversy often acrimonious. Of recent years O. W. Nixon, author of "How Marcus Whitman saved Oregon," and Dr. W. A. Mowry, author of "Marcus Whitman," have been among the leading popular exponents of the legend. Fortunately the subject attracted the attention of a trained historical student, Professor Edward G. Bourne of Yale, who examined the sources and subjected the evidence to a critical examination. In an address before the American Historical Association in December, 1900, he demonstrated the baselessness of the claim that "Whitman saved Oregon." Another student of the subject, Mr. W. I. Marshall, added some instructive testimony. For a final analysis of the subject the reader may consult Professor Bourne's address, which appears, revised, enlarged, and annotated, in his "Essays in Historical Criticism." An article by Mr. Marshall in the *School Weekly* of Chicago, February 22, 1901, cites the following authors of school histories as expressing themselves convinced of the falsity of the Whitman legend: H. E. Scudder, J. B. McMaster, W. F. Gordy, A. F. Blaisdell, and Mrs. A. H. Burton. He also quotes Edward Eggleston and John Fiske as at that time disavowing belief in the legend, which Fiske had accepted earlier from Barrows.

CHAPTER XXIV

THE COMING OF INDUSTRIES

The search for mineral wealth. Louisiana ignored for California. Later developments. The day of the "pony express." The great cattle industry. Opening of the interior by the first transcontinental railroad.

The treasure seeking of the Spaniards in the Southwest and various quests of the French belong to early history, but it was less than sixty years ago that Americans began to write the story of the mine in the West. A few pioneers knew something of the mineral riches of the West—trappers, scouts, fur hunters like Bridger, Ashley, or Peter Ogden famous in the annals of the Hudson Bay Company, or, later, William Sublette, Walker, and Kit Carson. These men had penetrated the mountains and knew the Great Basin. Some of them brought back tales of placer gold, and even showed specimens.

But it was not until 1848 that the age of gold was opened to Anglo-Saxons in the West. The digging of a mill race for J. A. Sutter at New Helvetia, California, brought the discovery of gold and the opening of one of the most eventful chapters in the record of the world's pursuit of mineral wealth. The Argonauts who crowded vessels bound for the Isthmus or the Horn, or painfully traversed the well-worn trails[1] from Independence or St. Joseph, made a history of their own. The number of men in the California gold fields rose from a handful at the time of the discovery to six thousand at the end of 1848, and thirty-five thousand by the close of the following year. Not until 1855 was a railroad opened across the Isthmus of Panama, but in the first twelve years of its existence it carried

---

[1]"Along this line [the overland trail] the 'prairie schooners' stretched for miles. . . . A traveler counted four hundred and fifty-nine wagons in ten miles along the Platte. . . . The cholera epidemic of 1849 carried off over five thousand of these immigrants gathered along the Missouri."—Sparks's "Expansion of the American People."

SUTTER'S MILL

eastward gold valued at seven hundred and fifty million dollars.

For this wonderful tide of overland migration the old Louisiana territory was but a country to be traversed. Yet the increased knowledge of the West had its influence, although the gold seekers neglected treasures which were developed later. The early fifties brought some beginnings of placer mining in Nevada and Utah, as did also the sudden and disastrous excitement over gold at Pike's Peak. The later fifties witnessed the discovery of the stupendous Comstock lode in Nevada, which was followed within a few years by the disclosure of mineral riches hidden within the confines of Louisiana. In the early sixties came discoveries of gold in Idaho and Montana, and later copper was added to swell an output beside which the initial cost of Louisiana sinks into insignificance, without reckoning the products of Dakota, the zinc and coal of Missouri, or the other mineral resources of a land crossed by the Argonauts with eyes open only to the gold of the Pacific coast. The first placers of Colorado were followed by the long list of discoveries which have given such names as

INDIANS ATTACKING THE " OVERLAND MAIL"

Leadville, Cripple Creek, and Creede a fairly historic character.

In 1803 a month and a half was required for the transit of letters from the eastern seaboard to St. Louis. Half a century later the best time for government dispatches from the eastern border of the old Louisiana territory to California was three weeks. In 1859 St. Joseph, Missouri, was the most western railroad point, two thousand miles from California. There were only wagon trains and stages over thirteen hundred miles of trail to the mountains and seven hundred miles of mountain roads. The plains were held by hostile Indians. For those who shrank from the privations and dangers of the overland trail there was left a choice between the Isthmus route and passage around Cape Horn. The need of quicker communication with California, which had been felt since the migration of gold seekers began, was made more imperative by political conditions. Out of this need grew the "pony express."[1]

[1]"Of all the expresses, the most romantic and picturesque was the pony express, inaugurated by William H. Russell and B. F. Ficklin in 1860, absorbed later by Wells, Fargo & Co., and abandoned in 1862, when the telegraph line was completed across the continent."—"The Story of the Railroad," by Cy Warman.

At the outset, as at the outset of most new departures, the idea was ridiculed. It was deemed impossible that a successful mail service could be maintained by relays of single riders over two thousand miles of practically

A "PONY EXPRESS" RIDER

business men assured the organizers of patronage. Some six hundred bronchos were purchased. A corps of seventy-five light-weight riders was enrolled, and relay stations were established at intervals of a hundred miles on the plains and forty miles in the mountains, each station equipped with a few men, several horses, and a generous supply of arms and ammunition.

At noon of April 3, 1860, came the opening of the "pony express" route, which was awaited on the Pacific coast with an interest second only to that caused by the driving of the spike which a few years later joined the Union and Central Pacific railroads at Promontory Point, Nevada. The pioneer rider started westward from St. Joseph, Missouri, followed by music and cheers, carrying a message from President Buchanan to the governor of California, with bank drafts, letters, and papers. The rider's distance was a hundred miles, and then his mail bag was carried on by his waiting relief.

So the mail sped on, across plains and alkali deserts, through cañons and over mountain passes, through the lands of a dozen hostile tribes, until ten days later the last rider reached Sacramento and the President's message was telegraphed to San Francisco. On April 3 also a rider started east from Sacramento with the first express pouch for the

East, which went through to St. Joseph in
eleven and a half days. This was the beginning of the "pony express."[1] Every week day
riders left St. Joseph and Sacramento. The
charge for letters was five dollars an ounce,
and later bonuses were paid for war news.
The fastest time was in December, 1860, when
President Buchanan's message reached Sacramento in eight and a half days from Washington. The news of the attack on Fort
Sumter came through in eight days and fourteen hours—two thousand miles. On the
western part of the route five riders were
killed by Indians, two were frozen to death,
and several were shot on the plains. One
man, finding the Indians had killed every one
at the relay station, rode two hundred and
eighty-four miles without rest, averaging sixteen miles an hour. Another covered two
hundred and eighteen miles with six horses,
one of which carried him seventy miles at

[1]"The Great Salt Lake Trail," by Colonel Henry Inman,
and Mark Twain's "Roughing It," afford some picturesque
sketches of the "pony express."

high speed. The "pony express" lived a life brief but crowded with thrilling episodes. It was ended in 1862, when the first telegraph line was built across the plains.

From the time of the "hunchbacked cows" of Cabeza de Vaca to the decade following the completion of the first transcontinental railroad, every traveler through the plains of Louisiana territory was impressed first by their extent, and next by the vast herds of buffalo. Then, they seemed countless. Now, the census of the handful preserved in the Yellowstone National Park and in private keeping can be taken all too readily. They were the mainstay of the flesh-eating Indians of the plains; but the slaughter by the Indians, barbarous as it was, counted as nothing beside that of the white hide-hunters and other merciless slayers—sometimes miscalled sportsmen. The completion of the Union Pacific Railroad divided the buffalo into the northern and southern herds, and ease of transit for hunters and the increasing pressure of newcomers hastened the work of extermination. The story of the buffalo forms a page melancholy but inevitable in the history of the West.

But the buffalo had their successors. The descendants of the Spaniards in Mexico owned cattle by the tens of thousands. Their cattle entered Texas,—sometimes by fair means, sometimes by foul,—and it was found that these sharp-horned, thin-limbed, muscular creatures throve on the buffalo grass of northern Texas. Seeing this, and eager for a market which did not exist in the distant Southwest, the owners drove the cattle northward. Even before the Civil War, Texas cattle were driven to Illinois. Soon after the war, experiments were made in driving cattle to Nevada, and even California was attempted. But the great route finally clearly marked out was almost directly north. It was found that the cattle gained weight in northern latitudes, and they were also brought nearer to a market. The opening of the first transcontinental road was an important factor. Thus the "Long Trail" was developed, as distinctive in its way as the

Trails worn by the pioneers, gold seekers, and emigrants.[1] In 1871, over six hundred thousand cattle were driven across the Red River toward the north. Out of all this grew the era of the cowboy and his reign from Texas to Montana. The cattle towns where he held his court when free from the labors of the drive or range afforded another distinctive page in the history of the West. But at length there came the invasion of settlers and farmers, the private ownership of land and water rights, and the opposition of barbed-wire fences. The "Long Trail" was ended, and the cowboy[2] of

[1] "The braiding of a hundred minor pathways, the Long Trail lay like a vast rope connecting the cattle country of the South with that of the North. Lying loose or coiling, it ran for more than two thousand miles. . . . It traversed in a fair line the vast land of Texas, curled over the Indian Nations, over Kansas, Colorado, Wyoming and Montana, and bent in wide overlapping circles as far west as Utah and Nevada; as far east as Missouri, Iowa and Illinois, and as far north as the British possessions."—Emerson Hough, in "The Story of the Cowboy."

[2] "There, jaunty, erect, was the virile figure of a mounted man. He stood straight in the stirrups of his heavy saddle, but lightly and well poised. A coil of rope hung at his saddle bow. A loose belt swung a revolver low down upon

the days of wild herding has nearly passed
away or is transformed into the milder herds-
man of a more closely regulated industry.

The great trails of the West were worn by
the feet of countless thousands for decades before the dream of a transcontinental railroad
took practical shape. But the idea[1] found

his hip. A wide hat blew up and back a bit with the air
of his traveling, and a deep kerchief fluttered at his neck.
His arm, held lax and high, offered support to the slack
reins so little needed in his riding. The small and sinewy
steed beneath him was alert and vigorous as he. It was a
figure vivid, keen, remarkable. . . .

"The story of the West is a story of the time of heroes.
Of all those who appear large upon the fading page of that
day, none may claim greater stature than the chief figure
of the cattle range. Cowboy, cattle man, cow-puncher, it
matters not what name others have given him, he has
remained—himself. From the half-tropic to the half-
arctic country he has ridden, his type, his costume, his
characteristics practically unchanged, one of the most dom-
inant and self-sufficient figures in the history of the land.
He never dreamed he was a hero, therefore perhaps he was
one. He would scoff at monument or record, therefore
perhaps he deserves them."—"The Story of the Cowboy."

[1]Mr. J. P. Davis, in "The Union Pacific Railway,"
mentions an editorial in *The Emigrant,* a paper published
in Ann Arbor, Michigan, as the first public expression of
the idea. But this was not until 1832. Various other

vague expression as early as 1819, when Robert Mills, in his book on the internal improvements of Maryland, Virginia, and South Carolina, argued for the connection of the Atlantic and Pacific by a steam road "from the head navigable waters of the noble rivers disemboguing into each ocean." Mills's plan, however, as shown by his memorial to Congress in 1845, was for a road for steam carriages rather than for a railway.[1]

Of all the early advocates of a transcontinental railway the most enthusiastic and persistent was Asa Whitney, a New York merchant, whose life from 1840 to 1850, and much of his later time, was spent in urging upon Congress, upon capitalists, and the public, the necessity for surveys and the benefits to be derived from a railroad across the continent. But any practical result from the

claims are recorded, including Senator Thomas H. Benton's declaration at St. Louis in 1844 that men full grown at the time would live to see Asiatic commerce crossing the Rocky Mountains by rail.

[1]Perhaps the reign of the automobile will yet show Mills a true prophet, though far in advance of his time.

surveys undertaken in the fifties was delayed by the Civil War and by the hesitation of private capitalists, and yet the war itself made plain the need of a railroad to the western coast. It was not until 1864, after the government had doubled its land grant and increased its inducements, that ground was broken at Omaha for the first transcontinental railroad. In 1869 the Union Pacific advancing from the East met the Central Pacific coming from the West, and the last spike was driven at Promontory Point in Utah, completing the first iron highway across the continent.

The Union Pacific presented some typical features which have never been surpassed.[1] In the abundance of Indians and buffalo on the plains, and of the thugs and thieves who invested Julesburg, Cheyenne, and other points with an evil reputation, the building

[1]Some features of this life are sketched in "The Story of the Railroad." "The Union Pacific Railroad," by John P. Davis, and Mr. E. V. Smalley's "History of the Northern Pacific Railroad," are useful for reference. A comparison of a map of the old trails and a recent map of the numerous transcontinental lines tells an interesting story.

COMPLETION OF THE FIRST TRANSCONTINENTAL RAILROAD
(Redrawn from a photograph)

of the Union Pacific held a certain preëminence. With this road began the work of the railroad surveyor and engineer in the true West, with its perils of all kinds on the plains and in the mountains, which forms in itself one of the epics of Western history.[1]

[1]Of this wonderful work of construction, Robert Louis Stevenson, in "Across the Plains," has given a vivid picture: "When I think how the railroad has been pushed through this watered wilderness and haunt of savage tribes; how, at each stage of the construction, roaring, impromptu cities full of gold and lust and death sprang up and then died away again, and are now but wayside stations in the desert; how in these uncouth places pigtailed pirates worked side by side with border ruffians and broken men from Europe, talking together in a mixed dialect,—mostly oaths,— gambling, drinking, quarreling, and murdering like wolves; how the plumed hereditary lord of all America heard in this last fastness the scream of the 'Bad Medicine Wagon' charioting his foes; and then when I go on to remember that all this epical turmoil was conducted by gentlemen in frock coats, and with a view to nothing more extraordinary than a fortune and a subsequent visit to Paris, it seems to me, I own, as if this railway were the one typical achievement of the age in which we live; as if it brought together into one plot all the ends of the world and all the degrees of social rank, and offered the busiest, the most extended, and the most varying subject for an enduring literary work. If it be romance, if it be heroism that we require, what was Troy town to this?"

CHAPTER XXV

PERMANENT OCCUPATION

The Free Soil issue. Kansas and Nebraska. Distribution of public lands. Louisiana in the Civil War. A glance at later development. Political and economic consequence of the old Louisiana Purchase.

The purchase of Louisiana was opposed by the New England Federalists. Half a century later their descendants were laboring to secure a result which would mean a political alliance with upper Louisiana. In the long struggle between the slaveholding and the free states the part of the Louisiana territory was one of supreme consequence.

By the act known as the Missouri Compromise, passed in 1820, Missouri was admitted into the Union as a slave state, but it was provided that there was to be no slavery in any portion of the Louisiana territory north of latitude 36° 30' except in the state of Missouri.

But by the middle of the century the westward movement of settlement reopened an issue which for a time had remained comparatively quiescent. In 1853, under the administration of President Pierce, it became clear that a new territory should be organized west of Iowa and Missouri, which would be within the Purchase. The North had believed the question of the extension of slavery into the Purchase settled by the Missouri Compromise. The South was fresh from the defeat of the "Wilmot Proviso," a bill forbidding slavery within the territory acquired from Mexico, and the representatives of the South were stimulated by the profits of slave labor on new land.[1] They were unwilling to see slave labor definitely excluded, but it was a senator from Illinois, Stephen A. Douglas, who introduced a bill providing for the admission of two territories, Kansas and Nebraska, and

[1] The influence of the cotton gin in cheapening production and the large returns from cotton raising by slave labor were obviously important political factors throughout this long struggle, and yet in the long run slavery was more expensive than freedom—a fact generally conceded now.

repealing the restriction upon slavery contained in the Missouri Compromise. Douglas argued that the Compromise had been superseded by the legislation of 1850, passed primarily with reference to the territory acquired from Texas, which declared a policy of "nonintervention"; that is, that new territories should be admitted without any regulation regarding slavery. In other words, they were to decide the question for themselves; and this idea, which was termed "popular"—and later "squatter"—"sovereignty," was embodied in the Kansas-Nebraska Act of May, 1854.

Out of this sprang a bitter struggle for control. It was a question on either side of the greater number of settlers. In Massachusetts, where men were not content with protests, there was organized an Emigrant Aid Society, and there were similar leagues in other northern states. The antislavery men strained every nerve to send settlers of their own party to Kansas, and with the coming of open strife the shipment of Bibles and rifles became a watchword of the times. Proslavery emigrants were sent from the South, and the Southern cause was aided from Missouri. The first election in 1854 was gained by the pro-slavery men. There followed the period of anarchy and civil war which made the name of "Bleeding Kansas" known throughout the land. But by 1858 the free-state men were in control, although Southern influence in Congress made it impossible for a time to gain admission as a state with a constitution forbidding slavery.[1] Nebraska, lying farther removed from the slave states, and rendered less important for a time by the preoccu-pation of settlers with the territory to her east, escaped the battle for free soil in upper Louisiana of which Kansas bore the shock.

This was but one of a series of events which stimulated the occupation of upper Louisiana. The California gold seekers, and others who

[1] It is unnecessary to give references to the voluminous literature of the slavery question which is readily accessi-ble. For the part which concerns this history, however, the reader will find it useful to consult "Kansas," by Leverett W. Spring, a volume in the American Common-wealth Series.

rushed to Pike's Peak in the fifties to find disaster instead of treasure, had passed by farming lands which were to enrich future owners by producing the food of America and of foreign lands. With convalescence from the California gold fever came appreciation of the farming lands of the middle West. While the battle for Kansas was in progress, a tide of immigration was sweeping into Iowa, which was presently felt in Nebraska and in Kansas as well. A telegraph line was built at Leavenworth in 1858, and two years more brought the opening of the first railroad in Kansas. To the north the development of Minnesota brought about her admission as a state in 1858. On the eastward, at least, upper Louisiana was developing its definite and permanent organization.

The vital importance of control of the Mississippi, which the history of the Louisiana Purchase illustrates so constantly, was shown again in the Civil War. Of the states formed within the Louisiana Purchase, Louisiana and Arkansas seceded from the Union. Missouri for a time seemed doubtful. Her decision influenced large issues not only from the size of the state and its position on the border, but also from Missouri's control of the Mississippi. Captain Lyon's seizure of Camp Jackson at St. Louis in 1861 represented an initiative action against secession which exerted an immediate effect. This was the first step in a struggle for Missouri which resulted in securing this strategical vantage point for the Union. It was in this struggle that Frémont, the "Pathfinder," proved himself more resolute as an explorer than as a soldier. After the earlier border warfare in Missouri and Kentucky came the great campaigns for control of the Mississippi and its tributaries, including Farragut's capture of New Orleans and a wonderful chapter of military and naval operations on the Mississippi and its tributaries. All this culminated in the surrender of Vicksburg to Grant on July 4, 1863, an event which ranks with Gettysburg as a turning point in the development of the war. The "great river" was returned to the control of the Federal government. The Confederacy was divided and its left flank turned. In President Lincoln's words, "the Father of Waters rolled unvexed to the sea."[1]

If the Civil War checked the process of permanent organization for a time, yet its close and the release of great armies of men to peaceful labors quickened immeasurably the development of the West. North and South met within the confines of upper Louisiana. Less picturesque than this reunion of veterans on the prairies but of large practical consequence was the increase of immigration from Europe which followed the ending of the war. To all possible settlers there were held out the tempting inducements offered by readily acquired land.

The history of negotiations with the original occupants of Louisiana, the Indians,[2] and

[1]This mere suggestion of the political and military consequence of the Mississippi in the Civil War, which is all that is possible in this history, may very well turn the attention of readers to "The Mississippi Valley in the Civil War," by John Fiske. Snead's "The Fight for Missouri" is, of course, more local in its interest.

[2]One view of our treatment of the Indians is presented in Mrs. Helen Hunt Jackson's "A Century of Dishonor." A comparatively brief study, largely from an ethnological

their subsequent treatment, is too often a history of mistakes and worse. A peculiarly difficult question was presented by the character of the buffalo-hunting Indians of the plains, who included Comanches and Lipans in Texas and Indian Territory, and Pawnees, Kiowas, Cheyennes, and the great Sioux tribe in the north. There were the Blackfeet and Crows west of the Sioux, and in Colorado were the Utes. These were the chief tribes of many with whom the government made treaties for the alienation of the lands which they had occupied, and for their retirement to reservations, in order that the wild country right be opened to settlement.

Whether or not the paternalism of the government was wise in its disposition of the public lands, its course stimulated the development of the Louisiana Purchase. By the

point of view, is afforded in the late Major J. W. Powell's discussion of the subject contained in "The United States of America," edited by Professor N. S. Shaler. For an understanding of the Indian on the personal side, there is no better popular work than "The Story of the Indian" by Mr. George Bird Grinnell.

Preëmption Act of 1841 any genuine settler could take up one hundred and sixty acres of public land and make his payments, on long time and easy terms, at a rate fixed in 1862 at one dollar and twenty-five cents an acre. The railroad land-grant system had its origin in 1835. The transcontinental roads received vast tracts of land along their lines. Over one hundred and fifty million acres were given to railroads between 1850 and 1870. The Union and the Central Pacific received twenty-five million acres, the Northern Pacific forty-seven million, and other roads obtained large amounts. So far as the government is concerned, the public domain has represented a loss; as regards the quickening of settlement and development and actual benefit to settlers, this disposition of public lands, with all its faults and flagrant abuses, has had certain practical advantages.[1]

[1]Donaldson's "Public Domain" may be consulted. There is a considerable literature dealing with the public lands, which has been increased of late years by such events as the opening of Oklahoma and Indian Territory, and the increased interest in national parks and forest preserves in the West.

In the case of the first transcontinental lines the railroad was pushed ahead of settlement. It was not a case of a demand for a railroad business due to increasing population, but an advance across long stretches of unoccupied country. Under ordinary circumstances it would have been wiser to advance the road step by step with the advance of population and of business; but in the case of the Union Pacific there was a necessity for a complete overland route. The Atchison, Topeka, and Santa Fé aimed at the mining business of Colorado, and, when checked at the Royal Gorge after an actual war with the Denver and Rio Grande, it turned southward through New Mexico, seeking a slowly realized outlet to the Pacific. The Northern Pacific, after a long and eventful struggle, was pushed through to Oregon in 1883, although at its opening it ran through long stretches of unoccupied country. For many of the transcontinental roads, granting the desirability of building them when they were built, the paternalism involved in land grants was a necessity. But there are features of this railroad building and of the government's distribution of the public domain which are creditable to neither side. All that can be said is, that, in spite of dishonesty, blundering, and waste, certain practical benefits have been realized and the settlement of the country has been accelerated. The part which the steamboat bore in opening and enriching the central valley of the West has been surpassed by the influence of the railroad in the development of the interior of the Louisiana Purchase—a development which without the railroad would have been impossible.

As to the later and comparatively recent history of the states formed within the Louisiana Purchase, the statistics provided in an appendix speak with a certain eloquence of their own. This narrative aims only to present a story of purchase and exploration, and the earlier phases of a domain less obviously a unit than the "Old Northwest" but peculiarly impressive and picturesque.

The history of Louisiana is crowded with possibilities fateful for the United States. In the struggle over the treaty of 1783, in which Spain and France were concerned as well as England, the United States refused to be confined to the eastern seaboard and secured an expansion to the Mississippi. Had the proposed restriction been enforced, it has been argued that a foreign power holding the whole middle West might have strengthened itself and alienated the American pioneers already beyond the Alleghenies, and have established a great colonial empire like that cherished by Talleyrand in his dreams. In the critical period of Louisiana after the Revolution there were possibilities of war with Spain and France and entanglements with England. It is profitless, perhaps, to consider past possibilities, and yet their consideration helps to measure the real significance of history.

The purchase closed a long contest for ascendency in the valley of the Mississippi. With the purchase the balance of power in the Western Hemisphere began to incline toward the United States. The acquisitions of Florida, Texas, California, Porto Rico and the Philippines, and presumably Hawaii as well, are termed by Professor F. J. Turner the corollaries of the Louisiana Purchase. "The Monroe Doctrine," to quote his words, "would not have been possible except for the Louisiana Purchase. It was the logical outcome of that acquisition. Having taken her decisive stride across the Mississippi, the United States enlarged the horizon of her views and marched steadily forward to the possession of the Pacific Ocean. From this event dates the rise of the United States into the position of a world power."[1]

On the economic side the acquisition of Louisiana meant first the ownership of a great system of water ways, whose control furnished

[1]Professor Turner's idea has an eloquence of its own, but with all deference to one whom every student of American history holds in high respect, it might be argued that there is a distinction between contiguous and practically inseparable Louisiana and the distant Philippines. A full recognition of the United States as a world power was apparently not brought home to European diplomats until the Spanish war.

the key that opened the interior of this continent. What that transportation was to the pioneer settlers west of the Alleghenies, to the fur traders of the interior, to the merchants of New Orleans and St. Louis, and to the development of the upper country, has been suggested in the course of this narrative.

The mineral resources of the purchase, ranging from the coal and iron of Missouri to the gold of Idaho, are indicated by statistics given elsewhere. It was the irony of fate that the Spaniards, whose keen scent for treasure was so richly rewarded in Peru, in Mexico, and even within our own borders, should have left Colorado practically unexploited and Montana unexplored.

An even more important part which Louisiana has assumed is that of the granary of the world.[1] The phrase is large but not uncalled

[1]Kansas leads the wheat-growing states with an acreage increased in forty years from 185,379 acres to 5,355,638. The production amounted to 82,488,655 bushels in 1900, while the second state, Minnesota, raised 51,509,252. In 1901 Kansas surpassed her own record with a yield of 99,079,304 bushels.

for. The vaguely described "American desert" of the middle of the nineteenth century has shrunk into narrower limits year by year with the pressure of settlement. The tilling of new lands has been accompanied by a palpable increase in rainfall, and the influence of irrigation, yet in an imperfect stage, has gained more and more land from a desert which is no longer feared. The present consequence of the wheat and corn of the Louisiana Purchase cannot be easily exaggerated. These cereals represent a question not only of food but of finance. Their success or failure is vital to great railroads and steamship companies, and influences the stock markets of the world. In other days cotton ruled as king, but the scepter has passed to the grain of the Louisiana Purchase.

Out of the productiveness of the Louisiana Purchase has grown an independence of mind as of estate. The lean years of subservience to Eastern capital have passed. The crumbling stock markets of 1903 found the West at first comparatively unconcerned, save for the effect upon the market for wheat, and occupied with its crops, its irrigation companies, and its development of local industries fostered by the money of its own people. The meeting of the Irrigation Congress, the influence of the Interstate Mississippi Improvement and Levee Association, the ways of expending national funds in the irrigation of desert lands, the possibilities of shipping southward by the Mississippi instead of eastward, and a thousand practical domestic subjects have maintained their interest in spite of Eastern absorption in the stock market. Years of bad crops may lie in the future, but the centennial year of the Louisiana Purchase has brought the development of an independence which can never wholly disappear.

Of greater consequence than richness of production is the effect of any great national undertaking upon the character of a people. In the acquisition of the vast plains, great rivers, and lofty mountains of Louisiana, there lay an influence more subtle than that of mere space and size. It was an expansion of our country which meant a larger character and broader outlook for its men. Whatever vagaries may have harbored temporarily in Louisiana in the past, its influence has supplied a manhood and a love of soil and country which crown the long, strange history woven through the centuries since the first coming of the Spaniard.

APPENDIX I

Treaty of Purchase between the United *States and the French Republic*[1]

The President of the United States of America, and the First Consul of the French Republic, in the name of the French people, desiring to remove all sources of misunderstanding relative to objects of discussion mentioned in the second and fifth articles of the Convention of (the 8th Vendémiaire, an 9,) September 30, 1800, relative to the rights claimed by the United States, in virtue of the Treaty concluded at Madrid, the 27th October, 1795, between His Catholic Majesty and the said United States, and willing to strengthen the union and friendship, which at the time of the said Convention was happily re-established between the two nations, have respectively named their Plenipotentiaries, to wit: The President of the United States of America, by and with the advice and consent of the Senate of the said States, Robert R. Livingston, Minister Plenipotentiary of the United States, and James Monroe, Minister Plenipotentiary and Envoy Extraordinary of the said States, near the Government of

[1]This treaty, which has been often reprinted, was officially published in the annals of Congress, 1802–1803, pp. 1006–1008, which give an official current history of the negotiations.

the French Republic; and the First Consul, in the name of the French people, the French citizen Barbé Marbois, Minister of the Public Treasury, who, after having respectively exchanged their full powers, have agreed to the following articles:

ART. 1. Whereas, by the article the third of the Treaty concluded at St. Ildefonso, (the 9th Vendémiaire, an 9,) October 1, 1800, between the First Consul of the French Republic and His Catholic Majesty, it was agreed as follows: His Catholic Majesty promises and engages on his part to cede to the French Republic, six months after the full and entire execution of the conditions and stipulations herein, relative to his Royal Highness the Duke of Parma, the Colony or Province of Louisiana, with the same extent that it now has in the hands of Spain, and that it had when France possessed it; and such as it should be after the treaties subsequently entered into between Spain and other States: And whereas, in pursuance of the Treaty, particularly of the third article, the French Republic has an incontestable title to the domain and to the possession of the said territory, the First Consul of the French Republic, desiring to give to the United States a strong proof of friendship, doth hereby cede to the said United States, in the name of the French Republic, for ever and in full sovereignty, the said territory, with all its rights and appurtenances, as fully and in the same manner as they might have been acquired by the French Republic, in value of the above-mentioned treaty, concluded with His Catholic Majesty.

ART. 2. In the cession made by the preceding article, are included the adjacent islands belonging to Louisiana, all public lots and squares, vacant lands, and all public buildings, fortifications, barracks, and other edifices, which are not private property. The archives, papers, and documents, relative to the domain and sovereignty of Louisiana and its dependencies, will be left in the possession of the Commissaries of the United States, and copies will be afterwards given in due form to the magistrates and municipal officers, of such of the said papers and documents as may be necessary to them.

ART. 3. The inhabitants of the ceded territory shall be incorporated in the Union of the United States, and admitted as soon as possible, according to the principles of the Federal Constitution, to the enjoyment of all the rights, advantages, and immunities, of citizens of the United States; and, in the mean time, they shall be maintained and protected in the free enjoyment of their liberty, property, and the religion which they profess.

ART. 4. There shall be sent by the Government of France a Commissary to Louisiana, to the end that he do every act necessary, as well to receive from the officers of His Catholic Majesty the said country and its dependencies in the name of the French Republic, if it has not been already done, as to transmit it, in the name of the French Republic, to the Commissary or agent of the United States.

ART. 5. Immediately after the ratification of the present treaty by the President of the United States, and in case that of the First Consul shall have been previously obtained, the Commissary of the French Republic shall remit all the military posts of New Orleans, and other parts of the ceded territory, to the Commissary or Commissaries named by the President to take possession; the troops, whether of France or Spain, who may be there, shall cease to occupy any military post from the time of taking possession, and shall be embarked as soon as possible in the course of three months after the ratification of this treaty.

ART. 6. The United States promise to execute such treaties and articles as may have been agreed between Spain and the tribes and nations of Indians, until, by mutual consent of the United States and the said tribes or nations, other suitable articles shall have been agreed upon.

ART. 7. As it is reciprocally advantageous to the commerce of France and the United States, to encourage the communication of both nations, for a limited time, in the country ceded by the present treaty, until general arrangements relative to the commerce of both nations may be agreed on, it has been agreed between the contracting parties, that the French ships coming directly from France or any of her Colonies, loaded only with the produce or manufactures of France or her said Colonies, and the ships of Spain coming directly from Spain or any of her Colonies, loaded only with the produce or manufactures of Spain or her Colonies, shall be admitted during the space of twelve years in the port of New

Orleans, and in all other legal ports of entry within the ceded territory, in the same manner as the ships of the United States coming directly from France or Spain, or any of their Colonies, without being subject to any other or greater duty on the merchandise, or other or greater tonnage than those paid by the citizens of the United States.

During the space of time above-mentioned, no other nation shall have a right to the same privileges in the ports of the ceded territory. The twelve years shall commence three months after the exchange of ratifications, if it shall take place in France, or three months after it shall have been notified at Paris to the French Government, if it shall take place in the United States; it is, however, well understood, that the object of the above article is to favor the manufactures, commerce, freight, and navigation of France and Spain, so far as relates to the importations that the French and Spanish shall make into the said ports of the United States, without in any sort affecting the regulations that the United States may make concerning the exportation of the produce and merchandise of the United States, or any right they may have to make such regulations.

ART. 8. In future and forever, after the expiration of the twelve years, the ships of France shall be treated upon the footing of the most favored nations in the ports above-mentioned.

ART. 9. The particular convention signed this day by the respective Ministers, having for its object to provide the payment of debts due to the citizens of the United States by the French Republic, prior to the 30th of September, 1800, (8th Vendémiaire, an 9,) is approved, and to have its execution in the same manner as if it had been inserted in the present treaty; and it shall be ratified in the same form and in the same time, so that the one shall not be ratified distinct from the other. Another particular convention, signed at the same date as the present treaty, relative to a definitive rule between the contracting parties is, in the like manner, approved, and will be ratified in the same form and in the same time, and jointly.

ART. 10. The present treaty shall be ratified in good and due form, and the ratification shall be exchanged in the space of six months after the date of the signature by the Ministers Plenipotentiary, or sooner if possible.

In faith whereof, the respective Plenipotentiaries have signed these articles in the French and English languages, declaring, nevertheless, that the present treaty was originally agreed to in the French language, and have thereunto put their seals.

Done at Paris, the 10th day of Floréal, in the 11th year of the French Republic, and the 30th April, 1803.

R. R. LIVINGSTON,
JAMES MONROE,
BARBÉ MARBOIS.

*A Convention between the United States of America
and the French Republic*

The President of the United States of America, and the First Consul of the French Republic, in the name of the French people, in consequence of the Treaty of Cession of Louisiana, which has been signed this day, wishing to regulate definitively everything which has relation to the said cession, have authorized, to this effect, the Plenipotentiaries, that is to say: the President of the United States has, by and with the advice and consent of the Senate of the said States, nominated for their Plenipotentiaries, Robert R. Livingston, Minister Plenipotentiary of the United States, and James Monroe, Minister Plenipotentiary and Envoy Extraordinary of the said United States, near the Government of the French Republic; and the First Consul of the French Republic, in the name of the French people, has named, as Plenipotentiary of the said Republic, the French citizen Barbé Marbois, who, in virtue of their full powers, which have been exchanged this day, have agreed to the following articles:

ART. 1. The Government of the United States engages to pay to the French Government, in the manner specified in the following articles, the sum of sixty millions of francs, independent of the sum which shall be fixed by any other convention for the payment of the debts due by France to citizens of the United States.

ART. 2. For the payment of the sum of sixty millions of francs, mentioned in the preceding article, the United States shall create a stock of eleven million two hundred and fifty thousand dollars, bearing an interest of six per cent. per annum, payable half-yearly, in London, Amsterdam, or Paris, amounting, by the half-year to three hundred and thirty-seven thousand five hundred dollars, according to the proportions which shall be determined by the French Government, to be paid at either place: the principal of the said stock to be reimbursed at the Treasury of the United States, in annual payments of not less than three millions of dollars each; of which the first payment shall commence fifteen years after the date of the exchange of ratifications: this stock shall be transferred to the Government of France, or to such person or persons as shall be authorized to receive it, in three months, at most, after the exchange of the ratifications of this treaty, and after Louisiana shall be taken possession of in the name of the Government of the United States.

It is further agreed that, if the French Government should be desirous of disposing of the said stock, to receive the capital in Europe at shorter terms, that its measures, for that purpose, shall be taken so as to favor, in the greatest degree possible, the credit of the United States, and to raise to the highest price the said stock.

ART. 3. It is agreed that the dollar of the United States, specified in the present convention, shall be fixed at five francs 3333-10000ths or five livres eight sous tournoise.

The present convention shall be ratified in good and true form, and the ratifications shall be exchanged in the space of six months, to date from this day, or sooner if possible.

In faith of which, the respective Plenipotentiaries have signed the above articles, both in the French and English languages, declaring, nevertheless, that the present treaty has been originally agreed on and written in the French language, to which they have hereunto affixed their seals.

Done at Paris, the tenth day of Floréal, eleventh year of the French Republic, (30th April, 1803.)

> ROBERT R. LIVINGSTON,
> JAMES MONROE,
> BARBÉ MARBOIS.

APPENDIX II

THE LOUISIANA PURCHASE TO-DAY

Its vast area. Statistical summary[1] of the states and territories formed from the Purchase. Fifteen millions of people. Wealth four hundred times the purchase money. The empire which we gained.

Figures are dry, but they can be helped by comparisons. The Louisiana Purchase contains 863,072 square miles, or 565,166,080 acres. This means an area more than seven times that of Great Britain and Ireland, and more than four times that of Germany. The Purchase is larger than Great Britain, Germany, France, Spain, Italy, and Portugal combined.

LOUISIANA

This was the first state formed within Louisiana territory.

I. AREA

45,420 square miles.

[1]From the Reports of the 12th Census and Yearbooks of the Department of Agriculture, except where otherwise stated. The 1900 census figures for agriculture are for the year 1899.

II. Population

Louisiana (1900) 1,381,625. New Orleans (1900) 287,104.
      (1810)   76,556.
      (1803)   49,475.   (1803)   8,056.

III. Agriculture and Manufactures

Louisiana is chiefly an agricultural state, the leading products being cotton, sugar, and rice. In the world's production of sugar the state holds third place, being led only by Cuba and Java. Sugar culture was introduced into Louisiana by the Jesuits in 1751. The phenomenal development of the rice industry in southwest Louisiana by means of irrigation has caused the construction of hundreds of miles of irrigating canals and the application of irrigation to more than one hundred thousand acres of prairie land which a few years ago had but a nominal value. These lands are now classed among the most valuable in the state.

In recent years manufactures, which were formerly practically neglected on account of the unfitness of slave labor for that form of production, have made considerable headway. In the years between 1850 and 1900, while the total population increased 166.8%, that portion of it dependent upon the manufacturing industries increased 579.9%.

In 1900 the value of manufactured products was $121,181,683, and the value of real and personal property was $189,099,050; the value of farm products was $72,667,302 in 1899, as against $54,343,-953 in 1890 and $42,883,522 in 1880.

The most important industries are sugar refining, lumbering, and the manufacture of cotton-seed oil and cake. An interesting feature of the sugar refining has been the establishment of large central refineries thoroughly equipped with the most efficient modern machinery. The planters, who used to do their own refining, now sell their raw produce to the refineries and are spared the cost of the installation and maintenance of refining machinery.

IV. PRODUCTS

Cotton (1900) 709,041 commercial bales (about 500 lbs.). Value $23,523,143.
(1890) 659,180 commercial bales.
(1880) 508,569 " "

Lumber (1900) value of product $17,408,513.
(1890) " " " 5,745,194.
(1880) " " " 1,764,644.

Timber cut in 1900, 1,214,387 (M feet, B. M.).

Rice (1900) 172,732,430 lbs. Value $14,044,489.
(1890) 75,645,433 "
(1880) 23,188,311 "

Cane (1900) 3,137,388 tons. Farm value $14,627,282.

Sugar (1900) 319,166,396 lbs. Value $13,099,559.
(1890) 292,124,050 "
(1880) 171,706,000 "

Syrup and molasses
(1900) 14,184,733 gals. Value $1,842,226.
(1890) 14,341,081 "
(1880) 11,696,248 "

Corn   (1900) 22,062,580 bu. Value $10,327,723.
            (1890) 13,081,954 "
            (1880) 72,852,263 "

Tobacco   (1900) 102,100 lbs. Value $20,488.
            (1890) 46,845 "
            (1880) 55,934 "

Sheep   (1900) 169,234.
            (1890) 186,167.
            (1880) 135,631.

Wool   (1900) 547,641 lbs. Value $90,317.
            (1890) 440,686 "
            (1880) 406,678 "

V. HISTORICAL EVENTS

1803. Napoleon sold the province of Louisiana to the United States.

1804. New Orleans was incorporated.

1807. Orleans territory was divided into nineteen parishes or counties.

1812. Louisiana was admitted to the Union, and that part of West Florida lying west of Pearl River was added to the new state.

1812. The first steamboat on the Mississippi arrived at New Orleans.

1815. The battle of New Orleans. Jackson defeated the British.

1831. The first railroad was opened in the state. It was four and a half miles long.

1861. Louisiana seceded from the Union.

1868. Louisiana was restored to the Union.

1879. James B. Eads completed his jetties in the South
      Pass, which opened the mouth of the Mississippi
      to vessels of the heaviest draught.
1880. Bureau of Agriculture and Immigration established.
1884. World's Industrial Cotton Exposition at New Orleans.
1890. Overflow of Mississippi River causes loss of $1,213,-
      040.
1902. East Louisiana and Southern Louisiana railways
      established. Total number of miles in state,
      2,898.

ARKANSAS

The name has been attributed to a compound of
French and Indian words meaning "Bow of smoky
water," and refers to the Arkansas River.

I. AREA

53,850 square miles.

II. POPULATION

(1900) 1,311,564.
(1820)   14,255.

III. AGRICULTURE AND MANUFACTURES

Arkansas is an agricultural state, but manufactures
are rapidly increasing. The principal products are
cotton, cereals, and tobacco. Fruit growing is very
successful, and the state is famous for its apples.

Arkansas is rated as one of the four states or territories having the greatest comparative gains in coal production in the past decade. Building stone is abundant, and a great deposit of liquid asphalt has been opened in Pike County. Beneath it has been found a stratum of fuller's earth. Some three thousand people are engaged in the pearl industry near Newport. There are also great zinc deposits in the state.

The manufactures of lumber and timber products are by far the most important. There are 1199 establishments, representing a capital of $21,727,710, which in 1900 gave employment to 15,895 wage earners, or sixty per cent of the wage earners of the entire state. The value of their product was $23,959,983, or fifty-three per cent of the value of all the products of Arkansas. The flour and grist milling industry ranks second, the manufacture of cotton-seed oil and cake ranks third, and cotton ginning is of fourth importance.

The value of farm products for 1900 was $79,649,-490, as compared with $53,128,155 in 1890 and $43,-796,261 in 1880.

The value of real and personal property for 1900 was $189,999,050. The value of manufactured products for 1900 was $45,197,731.

IV. PRODUCTS

Cotton   (1900) 709,880 commercial bales. Value $24,-671,445.

           (1890) 691,494   "   "

           (1880) 608,256   "   "

Corn (1900) 44,144,098 bu. Value $17,572,170.
(1890) 33,982,318 "
(1880) 24,156,417 "

Wheat (1900) 2,449,970 bu. Value $1,383,916.
(1890) 955,668 "
(1880) 1,269,715 "

Oats (1900) 3,909,000 bu. Value $1,263,101.
(1890) 4,180,877 "
(1880) 2,219,822 "

Hay and forage
(1900) 271,616 tons. Value $1,913,163.
(1890) 164,399 "
(1880) 20,630 "

Live stock (1900) value $37,483,771.
(1890) " 30,772,880.
(1880) " 20,472,425.

Sheep (1900) 168,761.
(1890) 243,999.
(1880) 246,757.

Wool (1900) 636,474 lbs. Value $118,922.
(1890) 512,396 "
(1880) 557,368 "

Milk (1900) 109,861,393 gals. Value of dairy products $6,912,459.
(1890) 54,325,673 gals.

Tobacco (1900) 831,700 lbs. Value $85,395.
(1890) 954,790 "
(1880) 970,220 "

Timber cut (1900) 1,665,158 (M feet, B. M.).

Lumber (1900) value of product $23,957,983.

Lumber (1890) value of product $8,943,052.

(1880) " " " 1,793,848.

Coal[1] (1899) 843,554 short tons. Value $989,383.

Flouring and grist mills

(1900) value of product $3,708,709.

(1890) " " " 2,498,168.

V. HISTORICAL EVENTS

1670. Arkansas was first settled by the French, near St. Francis River.

1812. Louisiana became a state, and Arkansas was included in Missouri territory.

1819. Organized as Arkansas territory.

1836. Organized as a state, Indian Territory being cut off.

1861. Seceded from the Union.

1868. Readmitted as a state.

1892. High-grade silver and lead ores were discovered about fifteen miles from Little Rock.

1898. Federal debt settled.

1902. 1,694 militia, regularly organized, uniformed, and in actual service of the state.

COLORADO

The Spanish gave the name of Colorado, which means ruddy or red, to the Colorado River. It is frequently called the "Centennial State," because it

[1]International Yearbook (1900). Census Report on Mineral Industries not issued. The product for 1899 is not representative, the production having been interfered with by serious strikes.

was admitted in 1876. The country was partially explored by Pike in 1807 and by Long in 1820. The discovery of gold brought a small army of treasure seekers to Pike's Peak and the surrounding country in 1859, and this began to draw the attention of the world to Colorado's vast mineral resources.

I. AREA

103,645 square miles.

II. POPULATION

Colorado	(1900) 539,700.	Denver	(1900) 133,859.
	(1880) 194,327.		(1880) 35,629.
	(1860) 34,277.		(1860) 4,749.

III. AGRICULTURE AND MANUFACTURES

Irrigation holds an important relation to Colorado agriculture; the soil is rich, but needs water to make it fruitful. Cereals and fruit are the chief agricultural products. Stock raising is an important occupation, but mining is the leading industry; gold, silver, lead, copper, and coal are produced in abundance. The state produces more than one third of the yearly output of silver in the United States.

The acreage irrigated in 1900 was 1,611,271.

The value of irrigated crops for 1900 was $15,-100,690.

The acreage of improved land under cultivation in 1900 was about 2,000,000.

1900. Value of farm products was $33,048,576.
1890. " " " " " 13,136,810.
1880. " " " " " 5,035,228.

The value of all manufactured products for 1900 was $102,830,137.

IV. PRODUCTS

Gold   (1900) 71,396 fine ounces.   Value $79,000,000.

Silver   (1900) 728,334 fine ounces.

Lead   (1900) 82,137 short tons. Value $49,937,006.

Copper   (1900) 8,000,000 lbs. Value $3,893,034.

Iron and steel
       (1900) manufactured product 232,815 tons.
       (1890)   "   "   30,207 "
       (1880)   "   "   4,018 "

Coal   (1900) 4,626,943 tons.
       (1880)   462,747 "

Coke   (1900) 503,543 tons.
       (1890) 199,638 "
       (1880)   18,000 "

Wheat (1900) 5,587,770 bu. Value $2,809,370.
       (1890) 2,845,439 "
       (1880) 1,425,014 "

Corn   (1900) 1,275,680 bu. Value $508,488.
       (1890) 1,511,907 "
       (1880)   455,968 "

Oats   (1900) 3,080,130 bu. Value $1,121,745.

Sheep   (1900) 1,352,823.
       (1890)   896,810.
       (1880) 1,091,443.

Wool   (1900) 8,543,937 lbs. Value $1,115,331.
           (1890) 4,544,332 "
           (1880) 3,197,391 "

Hay and forage
           (1900) 1,643,347 tons. Value $8,159,279.
           (1890) 714,555 "
           (1880) 86,562 "

Live stock
           (1900) value $49,954,311.
           (1890) " 29,675,528.
           (1880) " 15,927,342.

Dairy products (1900) value $3,778,901.

Milk   (1900) 38,440,111 gals.
           (1890) 19,680,761 "

V. HISTORICAL EVENTS

1852. Gold was discovered.

1857. Civilized Cherokees attempted to explore Colorado but were driven back by hostile Indians.

1858. Colorado explored at two points,—near Pike's Peak by a company from Kansas, and in the southwest by Georgians under Baker. Both found gold.

1859. Gold was discovered at Boulder Creek, Clear Creek, and Leadville. There were in the same year important discoveries of silver. The great discoveries of carbonate-silver ore at Leadville did not come until 1877.

1861. The territory was formed from parts of Utah, New Mexico, Kansas, and Nebraska.

1876. Colorado was admitted to the Union.

1878. Gold and silver production to date: 80 tons pure gold, 770 tons silver; and large quantities of copper and lead.

1891. The first passenger train ascended Pike's Peak.

1892. Pike's Peak set apart as a forest reserve. Gold found in large quantities in Squaw Gulch.

1893. Rich gold ores, yielding at rate of $120,000 per ton, were found at Cripple Creek in El Paso County.

1899. Southern Ute Indian lands opened to settlement.

1901. Colorado first in beet-sugar industry.

INDIAN TERRITORY

A part of Indian Territory was included in the Purchase.

I. AREA

31,000 square miles.

II. POPULATION

(1900) 392,060.

III. AGRICULTURE AND MANUFACTURES

Agriculture, grazing, and lumbering are the chief occupations. Indian corn and cotton are the principal products. It is estimated that there are twenty thousand square miles of coal fields. Since 1890 the manufacture of cotton-seed oil and cake has become one of the most important industries.

In 1900 the value of farm products was $27,672,-002, the value of manufactured products was $3,892,-181, and the value of real and personal property was $94,000,000.

IV. PRODUCTS

Corn   (1900) 30,709,420 bu. Value $6,999,018.

Cotton   (1900) 154,850 commercial bales. Value $4,-809,929.
        (1890)   34,115   "   "
        (1880)   17,000   "   "

Oats   (1900) 4,423,810 bu. Value $889,053.

Wheat   (1900) 2,203,780 bu. Value $1,121,259.

Hay and forage (1900) 480,609 tons.   Value $1,139,079.

Tobacco   (1900) 97,030 lbs. Value $10,284.

Live stock (1900) value $41,378,695.
        (1890) "   5,976,729.
        (1880) "   10,499.

Sheep   (1900) 12,648.

Wool   (1900) 50,711 lbs. Value $7,499.

Flouring and grist mills (1900) value of product $1,198,472.

Timber cut in 1900, 15,000 (M feet, B. M.).

Lumber   (1900) value of product $199,879.

Coal[1]   (1899) 1,537,427 tons. Value $2,199,785.

Coke   (1900) 24,339 tons.

[1]International Yearbook. Increase of over ten per cent in spite of strikes.

V. Historical Events

1832. Indian Territory, including Oklahoma, was set apart as an Indian reservation.
1834. Definite reservations were assigned to the five civilized tribes.
1838. The beginning of their gradual removal.
1892. The reservations of the Cheyennes and Arapahoes, having been ceded to the United States, were opened for white settlement.
1893. The Cherokee strip was opened and incorporated with Oklahoma.
1901. Opening of Kiowa, Comanche, and Apache reservations to white settlers.

IOWA

The name Iowa means "across beyond," and it was given by the Indians to a district west of the Mississippi, which formed part of Michigan territory and afterward of Wisconsin, becoming later the territory of Iowa.

I. Area

55,475 square miles.

II. Population

(1900) 2,231,853.
(1850) 192,214.
(1840) 43,112.

III. Agriculture and Manufactures

Iowa is one of the leading agricultural states, less than one per cent of the soil being unfit for cultivation. Meat packing, the factory manufacture of butter, cheese, and condensed milk, and flour milling are the principal manufactures. Coal is found under about one third of the state. An industry peculiar to Iowa is the manufacture of pearl buttons from the shells of fresh-water mussels found along the Mississippi and other rivers. The manufacture of lumber and timber products, which was once important, has now declined.

The value of all farm products for 1900 was $365,411,528, as compared with $159,347,844 in 1890 and $136,103,473 in 1880.

The value of manufactured products for 1900 was $164,617,877.

The value of real and personal property for 1900 was $2,106,615,620.

IV. Products

Live stock
        (1900) value $278,830,096.
        (1890) " 206,436,242.
        (1880) " 124,715,103.

Corn   (1900) 383,453,190 bu. Value $97,297,707.
        (1890) 313,130,782 "
        (1880) 275,014,247 "

Oats   (1900) 168,364,170 bu. Value $33,254,987.
              (1890) 146,679,289 "
              (1880) 50,610,591 "

Wheat   (1900) 22,769,440 bu. Value $11,457,808.
              (1890) 8,249,786 "
              (1880) 31,154,205 "

Potatoes (1900) 17,305,919 bu. Value $3,870,746.
              (1890) 18,068,311 "
              (1880) 9,962,537 "

Milk   (1900) 535,872,240 gals. Value of dairy products
                      $27,516,870.
              (1890) 486,961,411 gals.

Hay and forage
              (1900) 6,600,169 tons. Value $30,042,246.
              (1890) 7,264,700 "
              (1880) 3,613,941 "

Sheep   (1900) 657,868.
              (1890) 547,394.
              (1880) 455,359.

Wool   (1900) 5,015,965 lbs. Value $992,334.
              (1890) 2,649,652 "
              (1880) 2,971,975 "

Coal[1]   (1900) 4,645,481 tons.
              (1899) 5,177,479 " Value $6,397,338.
              (1880) 1,442,333 "

Slaughtering and meat packing
              (1900) value of product $25,695,044.
              (1890)   "   "   "   23,425,576.

[1]Statistical Abstract, 12th Census. Value of output in 1899 was the largest in the history of the state.

Flouring and grist mills
        (1900) value of product $13,823,083.
        (1890)   "   "   "   11,833,737.

V. HISTORICAL EVENTS

1833. The first permanent settlements were made at Dubuque, Fort Madison, and Burlington.

1838. Territory of Iowa organized.

1846. Iowa was admitted to statehood.

1855. The first railway was built in Iowa.

1856. The first locomotive to cross the Mississippi passed over the first railroad bridge across the river, between Rock Island and Davenport.

1857. The Spirit Lake massacre occurred, which greatly retarded the development of the state in the region of Okoboji and Spirit Lake.

1870. Geological Survey of State published.

1871. Corner stone for State Capitol laid at Des Moines.

1877. Canal around the Des Moines rapids opened. Length, 7½ miles; cost, $4,500,000.

1890. A rich lead mine discovered near Dubuque.

KANSAS

The first white men to enter the present limits of Kansas were Coronado and other Spanish *adelantados*. In 1804 Lewis and Clark, the American explorers, kept the Fourth of July on Independence Creek, near the site of the present city of Atchison. Three years later Zebulon Pike crossed Kansas to Colorado and discovered Pike's Peak.

The bloody conflict to keep Kansas a free state and to exclude slavery forms a thrilling chapter in our national history.

I. AREA

81,700 square miles.

II. POPULATION

(1900) 1,470,495.
(1860) 107,206.
(1854) about 8,000.

III. AGRICULTURE AND MANUFACTURES

Agriculture and grazing are the leading pursuits. The state is among the first in the production of wheat and corn. Tobacco, castor beans, and cotton are also important staples. Silk culture is becoming a notable industry. Horticulture is being successfully developed, and in 1900 there were over eleven million apple trees in the state. The chief industries are meat packing, flour milling, and car construction. Zinc is mined in large quantities, and coal underlies about a fifth of the state.

The value of farm products for 1900 was $209,865,-542, as against $95,070,080 in 1890 and $52,240,361 in 1880.

The value of manufactured products for 1900 was $172,129,398, and the value of real and personal property was $1,021,833,294.

IV. Products

Corn   (1900) 229,937,430 bu. Value $58,079,738.
        (1890) 259,574,568 "
        (1880) 105,729,325 "

Wheat   (1900) 38,778,450 bu. Value $19,132,455.
        (1890) 30,399,871 "
        (1880) 17,324,141 "

Oats   (1900) 24,469,980 bu. Value $4,915,896.
        (1890) 44,629,034 "
        (1880) 8,180,385 "

Potatoes (1900) 8,091,745 bu. Value $2,485,800.
        (1890) 8,242,953 "
        (1880) 2,894,198 "

Milk   (1900) 244,909,123 gals. Value of dairy prod-
            ucts $11,782,902.
        (1890) 201,608,099 gals.

Hay and forage
        (1900) 7,066,671 tons. Value $18,499,287.
        (1890) 4,854,960 "
        (1880) 1,601,932 "

Sheep   (1900) 179,907.
        (1890) 401,192.
        (1880) 629,671.

Wool   (1900) 1,599,374 lbs. Value $247,895.
        (1890) 2,253,240 "
        (1880) 2,855,832 "

Live stock
        (1900) value $190,956,936.
        (1890) "   128,068,305.
        (1880) "   62,704,149.

Slaughtering and meat packing
        (1900) value of product $77,411,883.
        (1890)   "   "   "   44,696,077.

Flouring and grist mills
        (1900) value of product $21,926,768.
        (1890)   "   "   "   17,420,475.

Coal[1]   (1900) 3,989,170 tons. Value $4,478,112.
        (1880) 763,597 "

Zinc   (1900) value of product $5,790,144.

V. Historical Events

1820. The first white settlements of any importance were made by Osage missionaries.

1854. The territory was organized.

1861. After prolonged conflict between the free-soil and proslavery parties, Kansas was admitted to the Union. In the same year the first overland stage-coach arrived at Leavenworth, seventeen days from San Francisco.

1874. Mennonites purchase 100,000 acres of railroad lands.

1877. Lead discovered in Cherokee County.

1889. Legislature appropriates $13,000 to encourage silk industry.

1898. Lands taken from Indians by United States restored by United States Supreme Court. Value $1,250,-000.

1902. 652 rural free-delivery routes in operation.

[1]International Yearbook.

MINNESOTA

The name means "cloudy water." About one third of Minnesota was not included in the Purchase. It is known as the "Gopher State."

I. Area

79,205 square miles.

II. Population

(1900) 1,751,394.
(1860)　172,023.
(1850)　　6,077.

III. Agriculture and Manufactures

Two thirds of the state are devoted to agriculture. Horticulture is an important industry, as is also stock raising. Flour and grist milling, lumbering, meat packing, and brewing are the most important occupations. Building stone is abundant, and Minnesota is at the head of the list for the production of iron ore.

The value of farm products for 1900 was $161,217,-304, as against $71,238,230 in 1890 and $49,468,591 in 1880.

The value of manufactured products for 1900 was $262,655,881, and of real and personal property $585,083,328.

IV. PRODUCTS

Wheat   (1900) 95,278,660 bu. Value $50,601,948.
               (1890) 52,300,297 "
               (1880) 34,601,030 "

Oats   (1900) 74,054,150 bu. Value $15,829,804.
               (1890) 49,958,791 "
               (1880) 23,382,158 "

Corn   (1900) 47,256,920 bu. Value $11,337,105.
               (1890) 24,696,446 "
               (1880) 14,831,741 "

Potatoes (1900) 14,463,327 bu. Value $3,408,997.
               (1890) 11,155,707 "
               (1880) 5,184,676 "

Hay and forage
               (1900) 4,339,328 tons. Value $14,585,281.
               (1890) 3,135,241 "
               (1880) 1,637,109 "

Milk   (1900) 304,017,106 gals. Value of dairy products
                        $16,623,460.
               (1890) 182,968,973 gals.

Sheep   (1900) 359,328.
               (1890) 399,049.
               (1880) 267,598.

Wool   (1900) 2,612,737 lbs. Value $460,305.
               (1890) 1,945,249 "
               (1880) 1,352,124 "

Live stock
               (1900) value $89,063,097.
                (1890) " 57,725,683.
               (1880) " 31,904,821.

Flouring and grist mills
         (1900) value of product $83,877,709.
         (1890)   "   "   "   60,158,088.

Timber cut (1900) 2,441,198 (M feet, B. M.).

Lumber   (1900) value of product $43,585,161.
         (1890)   "   "   "   25,075,132.
         (1880)   "   "   "   7,366,038.

Iron ore   (1900) 8,000,000 tons.

Iron and steel
         (1900) manufactured product 42,528 tons.
         (1890)   "   "   2,290 "

V. HISTORICAL EVENTS.

1680. The Falls of St. Anthony were discovered and
      named by Father Hennepin, the most important
      of the early explorers of the state.

1783. The part of Minnesota east of the Mississippi
      became United States territory by treaty, and
      was included in the Northwest Territory organ-
      ized under the ordinance of 1787. It was later
      part of Indiana, Michigan, and Wisconsin terri-
      tories successively.

1803. The lands west of the Mississippi came into pos-
      session of the United States by the Louisiana
      Purchase, and belonged successively to the terri-
      tories of upper Louisiana, Arkansas, Missouri,
      and Iowa.

1805. The expedition of Zebulon Pike furnished the first
       information as to climate, soil, and natural
       resources.

1818. Fort Snelling was founded.

1821. The first manufactory in Minnesota, a sawmill at Fort Snelling, was established.

1827. The first white settlers, Swiss refugees, appeared at Fort Snelling, and were allowed to cultivate lands belonging to the fort.

1849. Minnesota was organized as a territory.

1851. Twenty-one million acres of land were acquired from the Dakotas by treaty with Traverse, the Sioux.

1858. The territory was admitted as a state.

1860. At about this time a French millwright, M. N. La Croix, settled Faribault, and introduced the new process of flour milling which has since caused the prosperity of Minneapolis and spread over the United States. After its adoption large exports of flour were made from the United States, whereas previous exports had been in the form of grain.

1870. Northern Pacific Railroad begun.

1883. Completion of Northern Pacific Railroad.

1898. Outbreak of Indians at Bear Lake.

1902. Land values increased in a year from $5.76 to $9.78.

MISSOURI

This name formed two Indian words meaning "big muddy," and referred to the Missouri River.

I. Area

68,735 square miles.

II. Population

Missouri (1900) 8,106,665.   St. Louis (1900) 575,238.
        (1820) 66,587.
        (1810) 20,845.

III. Agriculture and Manufactures

The principal agricultural productions are cereals, tobacco, and fruit, horticulture being one of the most profitable occupations in the state. Stock raising and dairy farming are also extensively followed. The state has a vast wealth in manufacturing business, being one of the largest manufacturing centers of the country and holding the first place for tobacco manufacture. Meat packing, flour milling, and brewing are the leading industries.

The value of farm products for 1900 was $219,296,-970, as against $109,751,024 in 1890 and $95,912,-660 in 1880.

The value of manufactured products for 1900 was $385,492,784, and that of real and personal property was $1,093,091,264.

IV. PRODUCTS

Corn   (1900) 208,844,870 bu. Value $61,246,305.
              (1890) 196,999,016 "
              (1880) 202,214,413 "

Wheat   (1900) 23,072,768 bu. Value $13,520,012.
              (1890) 30,113,821 "
              (1880) 24,966,627 "

Hay and forage
              (1900) 4,062,199 tons. Value $20,467,501.
              (1890) 3,135,241 "
              (1880) 1,083,929 "

Milk   (1900) 258,207,755 gals. Value of dairy products
                  $15,042,360.
              (1890) 193,931,103 gals.

Sheep (1900) 663,703.
              (1890) 950,562.
              (1880) 1,411,298.

Wool   (1900) 4,145,137 lbs. Value $822,871.
              (1890) 4,040,084 "
              (1880) 7,313,924 "

Live stock
              (1900) value $160,540,004.
              (1890) " 138,701,173.
              (1880) " 95,785,282.

Timber cut (1900) 721,632 (M feet, B. M.).

Lumber   (1900) value of product $11,177,529.
              (1880)   "   "   "   5,265,617.

Tobacco[1] (1900) 3,041,996 lbs, Value $218,991.
           (1890) 9,424,823 "
           (1880) 12,015,657 "

Slaughtering and meat packing
           (1900) value of product $43,040,885.
           (1890) " " " 18,320,193.

Flouring and grist mills
           (1900) value of product $26,393,928.
           (1890) " " " 34,468,765.

Coal   (1900) 3,160,806 tons.
           (1880) 543,990 "

Iron and steel
           (1900) product of manufactures 100,001 tons.
           (1890) " " " 114,945 "
           (1880) " " " 112,284 "

Lead   (1900) value of product $3,852,435.
Zinc   (1900) value of product $2,011,724.

V. HISTORICAL EVENTS

1767. Pierre Laclède founded a trading post on the river,
and named it in honor of Louis XV.

1775. St. Louis had become a well-known fur depot and
trading station and had about eight hundred
inhabitants.

1804. Captain Stoddard of the United States army succeeded the Spanish commandant at St. Louis, and
the region was organized into the territory of
Louisiana. St. Louis was made the capital.

[1]While the production of tobacco has greatly decreased, the
manufacture has greatly increased.

1812. Louisiana became a state, and the name of the territory was changed to Missouri territory.
1817. The beginning of the Missouri Compromise agitation.
1817. The first steamboat arrived at St. Louis.
1821. Missouri was admitted as a state to the Union.
1822. St. Louis received a city charter.
1852. The first railway in the state was opened, with thirty-eight miles of track.
1873. Opening of tubular steel bridge across the Mississippi River at St. Louis, erected by J. B. Eads.
1901-1902. Expenditure of $900,000 in buildings for public institutions.

MONTANA

The name is taken from the French word for mountain.

I. AREA

145,310 square miles.

II. POPULATION

(1900) 243,329.
(1864) about 11,000.

III. AGRICULTURE AND MANUFACTURES

Agriculture is handicapped by need of irrigation,[1] the acreage under cultivation being 1,151,674, of which the acreage irrigated is 951,154. The value

[1]The greatly increased recognition of the importance of irrigation as shown in legislation, in appropriations, and in such action as the meeting of the Irrigation Congress in 1903, argues favorably for the increased utilization of Western lands.

of irrigated crops in 1900 was $7,281,567. Wheat yields about thirty bushels to the acre. Stock raising is an important occupation, and the state is one of the first in sheep raising and the production of raw wool. The chief industry of the state, however, is mining.

The value of farm products for 1900 was $28,616,957, as against $6,273,415 in 1890 and $2,024,923 in 1880.

The value of manufactured products for 1900 was $57,075,824, and that of real and personal property was $153,441,154.

IV. PRODUCTS

Oats	(1900) 4,746,231 bu. Value $1,790,938.
	(1890) 1,535,615 "
	(1880) 900,915 "
Wheat	(1900) 1,899,683 bu. Value $1,077,210.
	(1890) 457,607 "
	(1880) 469,688 "
Hay and forage	
	(1900) 1,059,268 tons. Value $5,974,850.
	(1890) 268,689 "
	(1880) 62,709 "
Sheep	(1900) 4,215,214.
	(1890) 2,352,886.
	(1880) 279,277.
Wool	(1900) 30,437,829 lbs. Value $5,136,658.
	(1890) 12,177,467 "
	(1880) 995,484 "
Live stock	(1900) value $52,161,833.
	(1890) " 33,266,752.
	(1880) " 9,170,554.

Copper   (1900) value of product $36,387,063.
Silver   (1900) coinage value $21,786,874.
Lead   (1900) value of product $5,264,253.
Gold   (1900) value of product $4,819,156.
Coal   (1900) 1,483,728 tons.
         (1880)   224   "

V. Historical Events

1827. Trading post established on the Yellowstone River.
1852. Gold was discovered.
1861. Discoveries of gold. The growth of the state dates from this time.
1864. Montana was organized as a territory distinct from Idaho territory, of which it had been a part.
1880. The first railroad entered Montana.
1892. The surplus lands of the Crow Indian reservation in southern Montana (about 1,800,000 acres) were opened to settlement.

NEBRASKA

The name, taken from two Indian words, means "shallow water." The state is often called the "Black Water State."

I. Area

76,840 square miles.

II. Population

(1900) 1,006,300.
(1860) 28,841.

III. Agriculture and Manufactures

Nebraska is an agricultural state, and ranks among the first for corn production. The sugar beet is an important product, and horticulture is very successful, apples, plums, and peaches forming the principal crops. It is one of the chief stock-raising and meat-packing states. The principal manufactures are farm implements, foundry products, flour milling, and sugar refining. The acreage of improved land in 1896 was 18,091,936.

The value of farm products for 1900 was $162,696,-386, as against $66,837,617 in 1890 and $31,708,914 in 1880.

The value of manufactured products for 1900 was $143,990,102, and that of real and personal property $171,747,593.

IV. Products

Corn (1900) 210,974,740 bu. Value $51,251,213.
      (1890) 215,895,996 "
      (1880) 65,450,135 "
Wheat (1900) 24,801,900 bu. Value $13,145,007.
      (1890) 10,571,059 "
      (1880) 13,847,007 "
Oats (1900) 58,007,140 bu. Value $11,333,393.
      (1890) 43,843,640 "
      (1880) 6,555,875 "
Hay and forage
      (1900) 3,502,380 tons. Value $11,230,910.
      (1890) 3,115,398 "
      (1880) 786,722 "

Milk   (1900) 190,477,911 gals. Value of dairy products $8,595,408.

(1890) 144,768,263 gals.

Sheep   (1900) 335,950.

(1890) 209,243.

(1880) 247,453.

Wool   (1900) 2,788,839 lbs. Value $426,344.

(1890) 791,534 "

(1880) 1,282,656 "

Live stock

(1900) value $145,349,587.

(1890) "   92,971,920.

(1880) "   40,350,265.

V. HISTORICAL EVENTS

1804. The Lewis and Clark expedition passed up the west bank of the Missouri. This was the first important expedition after the early Spanish and French explorers.

1810. The first settlement was made at Bellevue.

1849. The beginning of the great western movement of gold-hunters occurred, which incidentally established towns in Nebraska along the west bank of the Missouri.

1854. Nebraska was organized as a territory.

1867. The territory was admitted to statehood, the capital being removed from Omaha to Lincoln.

1869. The Union Pacific Railroad was opened for traffic.

1875. Present state constitution framed.

1902. Coal discovered near Jamestown.

NORTH DAKOTA

The name Dakota was taken from the general name of the Sioux tribes, and signified "many united tribes."

I. AREA

70,195 square miles.

II. POPULATION

(1900) 319,146.
(1890) 182,719.
(1860) 4,837.

III. AGRICULTURE AND MANUFACTURES

Agriculture is the principal occupation, and wheat is cultivated very extensively, great wheat farms of 20,000 acres being not uncommon. Horse and cattle raising is second in importance. The estimated area of grazing lands is 40,000,000 acres. The manufactures are for the most part domestic and local.

The value of farm products for 1900 was $64,252,-494, as against $21,264,938 in 1890 and $5,648,814 in 1880.[1]

The value of manufactured products for 1900 was $9,183,114, and that of real and personal property $143,000,000.

[1]Includes South Dakota.

IV. PRODUCTS

Wheat   (1900) 59,888,810 bu. Value $31,733,763.
           (1890) 26,403,365 "
           (1880)[1] 2,830,289 "

Oats   (1900) 22,125,331 bu. Value $5,852,615.
           (1890) 5,733,129 "

Corn   (1900) 1,284,870 bu. Value $397,278.
           (1890)   178,729 "
           (1880)[1] 2,000,864 "

Hay and forage
           (1900) 1,747,390 tons. Value $5,182,917.
           (1890) 531,472 "
           (1880)[1] 308,036 "

Sheep   (1900) 451,437.
           (1890) 136,413.
           (1880)[1] 85,244.

Wool   (1900) 3,030,478 lbs. Value $503,744.
           (1890) 510,417 "
           (1880)[1] 157,025 "

Live stock
           (1900) value $42,430,491.
           (1890) " 18,787,294.
           (1880)[1] " 7,555,274.

V. HISTORICAL EVENTS

1804 to 1806. Lewis and Clark explored the Dakotas, wintering near Bismarck, 1804–1805.

1830. The first steamer ascended the Missouri River into the Dakotas.

[1]Includes South Dakota.

1851. The first land was obtained from the Sioux Indians.
1861. Dakota territory was organized.
1889. North Dakota was admitted as a state.
1892. The Turtle Indians cede all right and title to lands
    in the Devil's Lake District.
1902. New military post established near Bismarck.

OKLAHOMA

In 1889 Oklahoma, up to that time an Indian reservation, was opened for settlement. From 1850, when as "No Man's Land" it was ceded to the United States, until its opening to white settlers, these unoccupied lands were the scene of perpetual struggle between the government troops sent to enforce the proclamations against settlement and organized bands of men determined upon taking up the lands. In 1901, 3,000,000 acres of Indian lands were opened. They now contain a population estimated at 80,000. Three counties have been organized, and the county seats have populations of from 8,000 to 12,000. The property of the settlers in this new country is estimated to be worth $9,000,000, according to the county clerks, on a basis of one third to one fourth real value. This showing for two years illustrates the rapid development of the last of the available new lands of the West. The total population of Oklahoma (1903) is estimated at 550,000, and with the Indian Territory added there would be about 1,100,000. The admission of these two territories into the Union as one or two states lies in the immediate future.

I. AREA

38,830 square miles.

II. POPULATION

(1900) 398,331.
(1890) 61,834.

III. AGRICULTURE AND MANUFACTURES

Agriculture, horticulture, and stock raising are the principal occupations, yet the increase in manufactures between 1890 and 1900 was more striking than that in any other state or territory.

The value of farm products for 1900 was $45,447,-744, as against $440,375 in 1890.

The value of manufactured products for 1900 was $7,083,938, and that of real and personal property $150,000,000.

IV. PRODUCTS

Corn	(1900)	152,055,390 bu.	Value	$48,037,895.
	(1890)	234,315 "		
Wheat	(1900)	18,124,520 bu.	Value	$8,989,416.
	(1890)	30,175 "		
Oats	(1900)	5,087,930 bu.	Value	$1,079,862.
	(1890)	76,194 "		
Cotton	(1900)	70,675 commercial bales.	Value	$2,217,119.
	(1890)	425 " "		

Hay and forage
        (1900) 1,137,296 tons. Value $2,883,682.
        (1890) 40,473 "

Sheep (1900) 48,535.
        (1890) 16,565.

Wool   (1900) 278,425 lbs. Value $37,750.
        (1890) 59,114 "

Live stock
        (1900) value $54,829,568.
        (1890) "   3,206,270.
        (1880) "   876,000.

Flouring and grist mills (1900) value of product $3,745,434.

V. Historical Events

1889. Oklahoma separated from Indian Territory and
      opened for settlement.

1890. Oklahoma territory organized.

1891. Cession of lands was made by Sac and Fox, Pot-
      tawattomie, Shawnee, Cheyenne, and Arapahoe
      Indians, which opened 300,000 more acres to white
      settlement.

1900. The governor claimed that Oklahoma was entitled to
      admission as a state.

SOUTH DAKOTA

This has been called the "Coyote State."

I. Area

76,850 square miles.

II. Population

(1900)   410,570.
(1890)   328,808.

III. Agriculture and Manufactures

Two thirds of the population are engaged in agricultural pursuits. Wheat, corn, and oats are the leading products, and stock raising is very profitable. Milling is an important industry, and the state is very rich in minerals, gold and silver leading.

The value of farm products for 1900 was $66,082,-419, as against $22,047,279 in 1890.

The value of manufactured products for 1900 was $12,213,239, and that of real and personal property $172,225,085.

IV. Products

Wheat (1900) 41,889,380 bu. Value $20,957,917.
         (1890) 16,541,138 "
Corn   (1900) 32,402,540 bu. Value $7,263,127.
         (1890) 13,152,008 "

Hay and forage
        (1900) 2,378,392 tons. Value $5,954,229.
        (1890) 1,541,524 "

Oats   (1900) 19,412,490 bu. Value $4,114,456.
        (1890) 7,469,846 "

Sheep   (1900) 507,338.
        (1890) 238,518.

Wool   (1900) 3,426,945 lbs. Value $525,652.
        (1890) 1,074,289 "

Live stock
        (1900) value $65,173,432.
        (1890) " 29,689,509.

Gold   (1900) 84,723 fine ounces.

Silver   (1900) 317,263 fine ounces.

Copper (1900) contents of matte 2,175,549 lbs.

V. HISTORICAL EVENTS

1857. The first settlement was made at Sioux Falls.
1861. Dakota was organized as a territory.
1872. The first railroad entered the state.
1889. South Dakota was separated from North Dakota and admitted as a state.
1890. The Sioux reservation, containing 9,000,000 acres, was opened to white settlers.
1892. The Yankton Sioux ceded part of their reservation between the Choteau and Missouri rivers.
1893. The state legislature passed an act to promote irrigation.
1902. Oil discovered thirty miles from Sisseton.

WYOMING

The name comes from an Indian word, and means "broad plain."

I. AREA

97,575 square miles.

II. POPULATION

(1900) 92,531.
(1890) 60,705.
(1868) 9,118.

III. AGRICULTURE AND MANUFACTURES

It is estimated that 12,000,000 acres can be made fit for cultivation by means of irrigation. The elevation of the state (average probably 6400 feet) also limits agricultural production, as cereals and other ordinary products of the section will not thrive above 7500 feet. Stock raising is the leading pursuit. Mineral resources are still to a great extent undeveloped. There are about 13,000,000 acres of coal fields, and large oil districts.

The acreage irrigated in 1900 was 605,878, and its value $2,886,949.

The value of farm products for 1900 was $11,907,415, as against $2,241,590 in 1890 and $372,391 in 1880.

The value of manufactured products for 1900 was $4,301,240, and that of real and personal property $37,892,303.

IV. PRODUCTS

Oats   (1900) 763,370 bu. Value $292,630.
(1890) 388,505 "
(1880) 22,512 "

Wheat   (1900) 348,890 bu. Value $191,195.
(1890) 74,450 "
(1880) 4,674 "

Hay and forage
(1900) 462,101 tons. Value $2,332,028.
(1890) 147,963 "
(1880) 23,516 "

Sheep   (1900) 3,327,185.
(1890) 712,520.
(1880) 450,225.

Wool   (1900) 27,758,309 lbs. Value $4,036,227.
(1890) 4,146,733 "
(1880) 691,650 "

Live stock
(1900) value $39,145,877.
(1890) " 18,785,301.
(1880) " 9,182,107.

Coal   (1900) 3,584,466 tons.
(1880) 589,595 "

Coke   (1900) 15,630 tons.

Iron and steel
(1900) manufactured product 9,422 tons.
(1890) " " 8,308 "
(1880) " " 8,741 "

V. Historical Events

1841. The first emigrant train for Oregon and California crossed Wyoming.
1867. Gold was discovered and Cheyenne city established.
1868. Wyoming territory was organized from Dakota, Idaho, and Utah.
1876. The battle of the Big Horn.
1890. The territory was admitted into the Union as a state.
1894. A rich gold strike is made in Dutch Tom Gulch.
1902. Completion of the longest aërial tramway in the world, extending from Battle Creek to Grand Encampment, a distance of sixteen miles.

The following table, based on the last census, sum-
marizes the area, population, and taxable property of
the states and territories of the Louisiana Purchase.

THE LOUISIANA PURCHASE IN 1900

STATES AND TERRITORIEES	AREA	POPULATION	WEALTH
Arkansas	53,850	1,311,564	$189,999,050
Colorado	103,645	539,700	430,000,000
Indian Territory	31,000	302,060	94,000,000
Iowa	55,475	2,231,853	2,106,615,620
Kansas	81,700	1,740,495	1,021,833,294
Louisiana	45,420	1,381,625	267,723,138
Minnesota	79,205	1,751,394	585,083,328
Missouri	68,735	3,106,665	1,093,091,264
Montana	145,310	243,329	153,441,154
Nebraska	76,840	1,066,300	171,747,593
North Dakota	70,195	319,146	143,000,000
South Dakota	76,850	401,570	172,225,085
Oklahoma	38,830	398,831	150,000,000
Wyoming	97,575	92,531	37,892,303
Total	1,024,630	14,887,063	$6,616,651,829

The Louisiana territory, once ridiculed as for the
most part a barren wilderness, now contains as many
inhabitants as there were dollars paid to make the
purchase.

The figures of the table show that the wealth which
is taxed is more than four times the amount of the
original purchase money. More than this, the splendid courage and energy shown in the development of
the territory, and the quality of the citizens whom
its opportunities have added to our country, represent
a value which is beyond price.

INDEX

www.ingramcontent.com/pod-product-compliance
Lightning Source LLC
Chambersburg PA
CBHW031230090426
42742CB00007B/135